Newly arrived immigrants at Castle Garden, New York
City (*Harper's Weekly*, September 2, 1865).

𝔗wentieth 𝔒entury 𝔏imited

How an Immigrant's American Dream Was Derailed by Corruption, Greed, and Politics

Emigrants boarding a North German Lloyd steamship in Bremerhaven, 1880. (Courtesy of Deutsches Auswandererhaus, Bremerhaven, Germany)

DOUGLASS C. HORSTMAN

iUniverse, Inc.
New York   Bloomington

Twentieth Century Limited
How an Immigrant's American Dream Was Derailed
by Corruption, Greed, and Politics

iUniverse books may be ordered through booksellers or by contacting:

iUniverse
1663 Liberty Drive
Bloomington, IN 47403
www.iuniverse.com
1-800-Authors (1-800-288-4677)

ISBN: 978-1-4401-6327-2 (pbk)
ISBN: 978-1-4401-6329-6 (cloth)
ISBN: 978-1-4401-6328-9 (ebk)

Library of Congress Control Number: 2009934578

Printed in the United States of America

iUniverse rev. date: 9/10/2009

To Elizabeth, Raymond, Caroline, and Abby:

In memory of your great-great-grandfather and his American Dream

America is an amazing natural experiment—a continent populated largely by self-selected immigrants. All these people had the get-up-and-go to pull up stakes and come here, a temperament that made them different from their friends and relatives who stayed home. Immigrants were the original venture capitalists, risking their human capital—their lives—on a dangerous and arduous voyage into the unknown.

John D. Gartner, *Washington Post*, April 11, 2006

CONTENTS

ILLUSTRATIONS

Emigrants boarding a North German Lloyd ship in Bremerhaven, Germany (cover).

Newly arrived immigrants at Castle Garden, New York City (inside cover).

Henry Christian Horstman.

Evangelical Lutheran Church in Hille.

The Horstmanns of Hille #29, 1884.

The emigrants' farewell.

Dispatch hall of the North German Lloyd in Bremerhaven, 1870.

S.S. Donau, North German Lloyd steamship.

Interior of Rotunda at Castle Garden.

Immigrants landing at Castle Garden.

Field hands cutting broomcorn in Glenville.

Schenectady Locomotive Works, 1890.

Cartoon displaying railroads' attitude toward workers' safety.

New York Central and Hudson River Railroad

Louisa Horstmann in a wedding photo.

Engineer Henry Horstman at Mynderse Street home.

New York's "Independent and Unfettered" U.S. Senator.

Advertisement in *Trainmen's Journal*, January 1903.

New York Central's *Twentieth Century Limited*.

Henry and Louisa Horstman; daughter Jessie.

Class F-3a locomotive.

Children of Henry and Louisa Horstman, 1903.

Class C-18 locomotive; New York Central's four-track main line.

German soldiers Heinrich and Christian Horstmann in 1915.

Horstmann farm (Hille #29), 1978.

Christian Horstmann and family at Hille farm, 1978.

Cousins Raymond Horstman and Heinrich Dreyer, 1985.

Horstman-Dreyer Family Reunion, Virginia, 1985.

Preface

This book is about my grandfather, Henry Horstman, a German immigrant who achieved his American Dream only to lose it in the prime of his life.

Piecing Henry's life together was a challenge. The demands of his work and raising a family left him with neither the time nor the inclination to pen an account of his youth in Prussian Germany, his journey to America, or his life on the railroad he loyally served. Any correspondence he had with his family in Germany has vanished and anyone who knew him has long since passed away.

Even my father, who was just three years old when Henry died, knew little about him. Henry's spouse, Louisa, an immigrant from the same village, couldn't bring herself to speak about her beloved husband after his death. She would say only that he was a good man who came home from work "exhausted, and covered in soot from head to foot."

Like many immigrants of the time, my grandfather had a life in America that was rooted in the railroad industry. His first job on the railroad allowed him to buy a simple, two-story frame house in Schenectady, New York, where I was born. That house witnessed several tragedies during my grandparents' lifetimes, some of which took place during my father's youth—events so sorrowful that my father would rarely speak of them.

But, as the saying goes, "what the son wishes to forget, the grandson wishes to remember."[1] Some tantalizing clues enabled me to begin unveiling Henry's enigmatic life. They included an old newspaper clipping about a train accident; a birth certificate from a Prussian church; a faded photo of a vintage steam locomotive; a polished brass bell; and a head-and-shoulders photograph of a handsome young man with sad eyes.

Although revealing, these fragments of his life couldn't answer some basic questions. Why did he come to America and how did he get here? What compelled him to become a *lokomotivfuhrer*, an engineer who drove the "iron horses" of the day? How did he adapt to life in an American industrial city? And most important, what precipitated his untimely death? Answering the latter question revealed widespread corruption in the railroad industry and unprecedented carnage on the nation's railways.

I traveled to the present German state of North Rhine-Westphalia, where I found descendants of his family still living on the farm where he was born. I also visited Schenectady, a once-great locomotive manufacturing center, where his dream to become an engineer came to fruition on the New York Central and Hudson River Railroad. Trainmen like Henry, many of them immigrants, went about their jobs without complaint while they faced unimaginable dangers on the rails. Henry was one of more than 46,000 railroad workers killed or injured on the job in a single year, a staggering number of casualties that exceeds the total casualties incurred by the U.S. armed forces in 6 years of the present-day Iraq War.[2] These unsung heroes were vital contributors to our nation's railroading history, described by one author as "the most heroic of American legends."[3]

The principal purpose of this book is to preserve my grandfather's *lebengeschichte* (life story). But it also aims to pinpoint the widespread corruption in the railroad industry that undermined the lives and livelihoods of so many "men of the rails." Peeling back the layers of his extraordinary story was like trying to peel an onion without shedding tears.

Henry Christian Horstman

Prologue:
A Disastrous Year

On September 27, 1903, a Southern Railway train known as the *Fast Mail* headed down a steep grade toward a seventy-five-foot-tall trestle that spanned Cherrystone Creek near Danville, Virginia.

The engineer, who was trying to make up time to be on schedule, was running too fast and was unable to slow the train as he approached the trestle. In one of the most spectacular and most remembered railroad accidents of all time, the entire train plunged into a ravine, killing the entire crew and a number of mail clerks working on the train. Headlines across the country spotlighted the terrible accident and inspired a railroad ballad called "The Wreck of the Old 97."[1]

Predictably, the railroad, which had a high-paying contract with the U.S. Post Office to carry mail, blamed the engineer. The luckless engineman had known the contract had a penalty clause for each minute the train was late and had been under pressure from his bosses to stay on time in order to avoid penalties. He and his crew were among 3,367 railroad workers who were killed on the job in a one-year period. At the same time, another 43,266 were injured.[2]

Six days after this disaster, another engineer was at the helm of a slow-moving "pickup," or local freight train. Henry Horstman was running east on the New York Central and Hudson River line toward his scheduled destination, the railroad's West Albany Yard. Like every engineman on the road, he surely had news of the *Fast Mail* accident on his mind. Any trainman worth his salt would be thinking about it and taking special precautions.

Henry had arrived on America's shores at the age of seventeen, one of 200,000 Germans who braved the Atlantic Ocean to come here in 1881.[3] Like many other immigrants, he found work on America's fast-growing railroads. But the railroads made it clear that men who worked for them did so at their own risk. It was the most dangerous industry in the nation and trainmen—engineers, firemen, brakemen, and conductors—bore the brunt of the casualties.

Engineer Horstman had every reason to be cautious. Married with four children, he was living his boyhood dream to become a locomotive engineer. It hadn't been an easy goal to achieve. For ten years, the German-born immigrant had labored as a fireman assigned to the back-breaking job of shoveling coal into the ravenous boilers of the railroad's steam-driven locomotives. Finally, he had won promotion to the engineer's side of the cab. With five years' experience at the throttle, he hoped someday to head up a fast express like the sleek *Twentieth Century Limited,* a luxurious passenger train launched by the New York Central a year earlier.

Saturday, October 3 was a crisp fall day in upstate New York. The young engineman adroitly maneuvered his freight train in and out of sidings at freight houses in the small towns and villages that populated the Mohawk Valley. Driving a local freight was a not-very-glamorous and grueling job that usually fell to engineers like Henry who were relatively low on the railroad's seniority scale.

It's more than likely that Henry was dog-tired as he coaxed his aging locomotive toward its journey's end, about thirty-five miles distant. The railroad's freight bosses pushed crews relentlessly to boost tonnage delivered on the line. Men worked day and night, often well beyond the normal ten-to-twelve-hour workday. Henry looked forward to getting home to his family. His wife, Louisa, was already planning a celebration for his fortieth birthday, little more than two weeks ahead.

As the usually slow-moving train neared Tribes Hill, a town just west of Amsterdam, New York, Henry moved from the engine's cab onto the gangway. What happened next is not clear except that without warning he tumbled from the engine onto an adjoining track. By the time his crew brought the cinder-spewing locomotive to a screeching halt and rushed to his side, he was unconscious but still alive.

It was a simple yet inexplicable accident that would resonate for years to come. As Roger Daniels writes in his *Coming to America,* many European immigrants arrived on our shores looking "to partake in an adventure, a drama, even a dream."[4] But sometimes, he notes, the immigrant's dream turned into a nightmare. So it was with Henry Horstman.

His story begins in a tiny nineteenth-century Prussian village.

One

HOMELAND WITHOUT HOPE

*The great questions of our time will not be decided by speeches
and majority resolutions ... but by blood and iron.*

Otto von Bismarck, September 30, 1862[1]

Seventeen-year-old Henry (Heinrich) Horstmann had seen it happen
many times in his village, a Prussian hamlet named Hille near
the city of Minden in Westphalia. Military police, easily identified by
their *pickelhaube* (spiked helmets), would suddenly show up to round
up eligible males. First they examined birth records in the village
church to identify those eighteen years of age and older. Then they
would confront a reluctant *Junge*, demanding that he report to a nearby
military unit or face arrest.

That prospect was not appealing to Henry, whose older brother,
Christian, had been conscripted into the German Army some two years
earlier. Conscripts into the Prussian guard faced tough training and
sometimes brutal treatment as they became grenadiers, fusiliers, or
Schützen (sharpshooters) in the infantry. Henry would soon turn eighteen
and knew that he, too, was a prime prospect for the army. Little time was
left before the police would come knocking on his door.

Born on October 21, 1863,[2] on a farm in Hille known as #29,
Henry lived during the time when Otto von Bismarck, the prime

minister of Prussia, launched a series of successful but bloody victories known as the "Wars of Unification." Bismarck's rise to power triggered an upheaval on the scale of the Civil War in America that took the lives of thousands of young Prussian soldiers. His stunning victories over Austria in 1866 and France in 1871 paved the way for a powerful new German Empire under King Wilhelm I of Prussia. A national hero, Bismarck intended to maintain German's military supremacy over its neighbors. Under the "Iron Chancellor," Germany's first duty was to be strongly armed, and no one was as important as the soldier.

As Henry grew up, Hille's population varied little from the 2,092 inhabitants who lived there in 1873.[3] When identifying themselves, villagers would always start with their *Heimat* (hometown): "I was born in Hille, Kreis Minden," they would say. It was an indication of how important the village and its parish were to their existence—it was a place where they were connected by ties of blood, and kinship carried heavy weight. At least six different households in Hille were headed by a Horstmann,[4] a common name in the village and in surrounding hamlets like Eickhorst, Hartum, Holzhausen, Sudhemmern, and Nordhemmern.

It was a time of unrelenting poverty in the village. Farmers eked out their livings from the poor soil as cheap grain imports from the American Midwest, some produced by German-born farmers, triggered an agricultural depression. Other villagers survived by growing, spinning, and weaving flax and linen but were unable to compete with goods produced on looms, or with cheap cotton flooding in from England.[5]

Henry's mother, Caroline, prepared food and clothing for the family. Children were expected to assist in the work required to run the farm and were assigned tasks suitable for their age and physical condition. Christian, Henry's father, was the undisputed head of the Horstmann family at Hille #29. In a typical Prussian family, it was understood that children were to obey their elders—particularly their father. He made all vital decisions and was the family's primary source of discipline and authority. He was in charge of the fields, and it was his moral obligation to keep the land intact for those who lived on it and for their descendants.[6]

Farmers like the Horstmanns at Hille #29 were known to share many traits in common. According to noted historian Oscar Handlin, "Thrifty, hard-working, and disciplined, the Germans preferred to exhaust their own bodies rather than the soil. The women and children toiled long hours, as did the men; and more effort went into the construction of barns and the care of animals than on comforts for the home or on the fripperies of dress."[7]

Under a centuries-old custom, *Anerbenrecht*, land was inherited by the oldest son in a family. It was also customary that when the oldest son married he would bring his bride home where they lived until his father retired or died and he inherited the land. These timeworn practices guaranteed that Henry had no future on the land where he was being raised.

During the turbulent Bismarck era, life in Hille was punctuated by random episodes of hunger, sickness, and death. Few of the villagers were spared the loss of loved ones, including Henry's parents. Married in 1859, Christian and Caroline (Kasten) Horstmann produced twelve children, five of whom survived no more than five years. Their childrens' deaths were a tragic outcome of the sicknesses and disease that swept through European villages and towns like Hille. "Sadness was the tone of life, and death and disaster no strangers," writes Handlin, chronicler of the great European migration to America.[8]

Before he was eight years old, Henry endured the loss of a brother and a sister. By the time he turned fourteen, two more sisters had died. The loss of so many family members undoubtedly left a deep and lasting impression on him. As he matured, he began to ponder what the future held for a poor farm boy living on land that his older brother would inherit.

Hille's Evangelical Lutheran Church, a presence in the village since 1523, was a place of stability where the Horstmann family and other villagers could turn in times of crisis. It provided comfort and a conscience in the face of recurrent sickness and death. Its pastor,

Hilmar Sasse, led a revival movement called the "awakening" that strongly influenced the villagers' daily lives.[9] Faith, the church taught, was the only way by which man could receive God's grace. Man's lot was to suffer and to atone for his sins which meant that he looked to the afterlife rather than a present that was filled with nothing but trouble and sorrow.

The Hille church was also a clear link to the past. Since 1726, its pastors had faithfully recorded major events in their parishioners' lives. Their handwritten entries in the church books noted every birth, marriage, or death that took place in the village, including at least four generations of Horstmanns who lived at Hille #29.[10]

Johann Heinrich Horstmann was the earliest of Henry's ancestors to occupy Hille #29. He apparently inherited or acquired the farm in 1752.[11] According to village tax records, Hille #29 was a medium sized property at the time, amounting to about six hectares (about fifteen acres) and consisted of a field, a meadow, and a garden. Church records show that his son, Johann Cord Horstmann, was born at Hille #29 on May 8, 1773, and eventually inherited the property.

The Hille church also organized the village's elementary school, one of many *Volksschulen* in Prussia that provided eight years of basic education. Henry's day at the straw-roofed, one-room school (all classes met there) began with religious instruction and continued with reading, writing, arithmetic, and singing. Schoolmaster Fritz Haverkamp taught traditional Prussian virtues like hard work, respect for law and order, good manners, and obedience to authority.[12] Lessons were taught in *Platt Deutsch*, or low German, a dialect still spoken in the region today.

It was not possible for Henry to go beyond this basic education. The Prussian education system was intentionally structured to make it difficult to get higher education.[13] The theory was that the "masses" should be kept in their place. The way to higher education was through the Gymnasium, which was a costly route and out of the reach of the lower and middle classes. It was a system designed to place the burden of military service on the poor and less educated.

Evangelical Lutheran Church, Hille, Kreis Minden, ca. 1900.

When Henry was ten years old, his father constructed a new farmhouse with the help of Meister Pohlmann, a master craftsman in Hille. Connected to a barn, *der Bauernhaus* had a steep red-tiled roof with a wooden beam over its front entrance. Carved into the beam was an inscription:

Christian Friedrich Horstmann und Caroline Marie Horstmann geb. Kasten haben dieses haus am 10 Juni im Jahre 1874 erbaut.[14]

In 1875, rumors of another war with France erupted. "Is War in Sight?" asked the *Berliner Post* as German newspapers warned that France sought revenge for its humiliating defeat at the hands of the Prussians. Bismarck convinced the Reichstag to extend a draft law for seven years. Under the German Empire's military law, all able-bodied men were required to serve on active duty for three years, followed by four years in the active reserves.

Finished with his required schooling, fourteen-year-old Henry took on a bigger role on the farm. His father relied heavily on him and his older brother to help in planting, bringing in the harvests, and tending the animals that were their main sources of food. A poor harvest of grain or potatoes, or an unexpected loss of livestock, could mean long stretches without food for the family. They worked in the fields trying to coax better yields from the wheat, rye, and potato crops that grew sporadically in the overworked soil. When his brother left for the army, Henry became his father's right-hand man. The demanding work imbued the young farmhand with a deeply ingrained work ethic and a determination to improve his lot in life.

Henry had little time to see life beyond Hille and its steep-roofed, half-timbered houses except when he rode with his father to Minden, about fifteen kilometers distant. Traveling over the countryside in a horse-drawn wagon, they passed windmills with canvas sails spinning in the wind, wooden *Boch* mills standing on their pedestals, and horse-powered mills grinding corn into flour. Before crossing a bridge over the Weser River into the city, they could stop at the Minden Bahnhof, a huge railway station and the oldest one in Germany.[15] Thundering locomotives barreled down the track, their wheels pounding the rails as the steam-driven, *Borsig*-built engines spewed plumes of smoke and sparks. Passenger trains ran to places like Cologne and Berlin, cities Henry had never seen. To the young onlooker, the *lokomotivfuhrer* who sat high in the locomotive's cab was a bigger-than-life, fearless figure.

Henry's father was raised at Hille #29 with two brothers, Friedrich and Carl, who emigrated to America many years earlier. Their letters from America were surely heartening as both brothers were clearly succeeding in their new homeland. Friedrich had become a *lokomotivfuhrer* heading up express trains and Carl actually owned his own farm. It was Friedrich, the uncle who drove the iron horses, who captured Henry's imagination and planted the seed of his American Dream.

As the 1880s began, a military bill backed by Bismarck gave Germany a peacetime army of half a million men and extended time of service in the *Landwehr* (reserves) so that another 700,000 could be called up. And if war broke out, Bismarck was authorized to double the size of the German army, putting one million men on the country's eastern and western borders.[16]

In the spring of 1881, Henry knew that before the year's end the military police would be asking about him. Under the German Empire's military law, conscripts served three years and then were passed on to a reserve unit for a seven-year period.[17] But even if he served a stint in the army, he couldn't envision a future in Hille. There was no question that his older brother (named Christian after his father) would eventually inherit the farm. Henry and his younger brother (Fred) were expected to find work on their own when they came of age even though the widespread economic depression provided no hope that a young man could improve his status in life.[18]

Faced with similar circumstances a generation earlier, Henry's two uncles had chosen to take their chances in America. It had worked out well. With a hand from uncle Friedrich, perhaps Henry, too, could become a *lokomotivfuhrer* in the land of opportunity across the ocean. But it would mean leaving—probably forever—his family and friends, as well as his ties to the land where at least four generations of Horstmanns before him had been born. That would be a gutsy decision for a boy not yet eighteen years old.

Henry's brother Christian (1861–1926) stands at center with parents Christian F. Horstmann (1832–1897) and Caroline (Kasten) Horstmann (1839–1894). Other children, from left, are Sophie, Marie, Caroline, and Frederika. Missing from photo are Henry and his younger brother Fred, who emigrated to America in 1881 and 1883, respectively.

Two

AUF WIEDERSEHEN

He would leave now, escape; give up this abusive land his fathers
had never mastered. He would take up what remained and never
see the sight of home again. He would become a stranger on the
way, pack on back ... toward some other destiny. For all about was
evidence of the consequences of staying. Any alternative was better.

Oscar Handlin, *The Uprooted*[1]

As children, Henry's parents were survivors of a deadly "potato rot" that spread throughout Europe, especially Ireland, in the 1840s. Potatoes were the main source of food in rural villages like Hille and Eickhorst, the latter where Henry's mother was born. Between 1845 and 1850, the potato-killing fungus, combined with a poor wheat and rye harvest, caused an estimated 42,000 Prussians to die from starvation and famine-related diseases.[2]

Enticed by promises of good jobs and fertile land in America, Christian Horstmann's two younger brothers, who by tradition were not in line to inherit the family property, joined a tidal wave of emigrants who left their homeland in the mid 1850s. Friedrich and Carl settled in upstate New York where a small but growing community of Hille emigrants had taken up residence.

An earlier generation of the Hille Horstmann family had also lived a miserable existence. Johann and Margretha (Wehmers) Horstmann were raising *kinder* at Hille #29 when Napoleon's troops occupied Westphalia. Thousands of French soldiers quartered throughout the region lived and ate at the people's expense and forced them to supply fixed numbers of troops for Napoleon's *Grande Armée*.[3] An unsuccessful revolt against the French in 1809 left few Prussian survivors, one named Wilhelm Horstmann.[4]

Not long after Napoleon's occupation ended, the region was hammered by an agricultural catastrophe. Dams burst and river valleys flooded. The fall harvest in 1816 was wiped out by snow; villagers dug through it to find frozen and rotten potatoes. By winter, people were subsisting on grass and roots while the most desperate even tried to make bread out of wood. Thousands of people left their homes, fleeing to North America and Russia, in the worst agricultural disaster in memory.[5]

Church records show that Johann, "the farmer from Hille #29," lost his wife to starvation. Their eldest son, Carl Heinrich Horstmann, survived both Napoleon and the 1816 disaster. He married Elizabeth Kleine in 1824 and brought her to Hille #29 where they produced seven children, among them Henry's father, Christian.

No doubt, this family history was on Christian's mind in 1881 when his second son was faced with the prospect of conscription into the army. Henry's father likely served in the Prussian Army at a time when soldiers were used as mere cannon fodder. One account described soldiers as "tortured creatures" who were fed only one loaf of black bread every five days.[6] No father would wish that on a son.

Christian recognized there was no future for Henry in Hille, as his firstborn son would inherit the farm. For the same reason, Christian's own younger brothers had left home many years earlier. Many Hille villagers had settled in upstate New York where they found jobs that paid well and fertile farmland along a river called the Mohawk.

Now another family member at Hille #29 was faced with the choice of a bleak future at home or a fresh start in a promising new land. As difficult as it must have been, Henry's father gave his son the nod to leave his homeland and break out of the cycle of hopelessness that had afflicted so many generations of Horstmanns. He would not derail Henry's dream to become a *lokomotivfuhrer* in America.

Sometime during the winter of 1880–81, Christian Horstmann wrote to his brothers in America. Would they look after Henry if he came to Schenectady? Christian was not able to pay for the boy's passage as the farm produced barely enough to sustain the family. The price for a steamship ticket across the Atlantic Ocean from Bremen to New York was 120 *Reichsmarks* (about $28),[7] a princely sum for a poor Hille farmer. The average per capita income in Germany was only 373 *Reichsmarks*, or about $87 a year.[8]

Perhaps recalling his own experience, Friedrich offered to help Henry find work and a place to live. As a senior engineer on the New York Central and Hudson River Railroad, he earned as much as $100 a month. It's likely he also provided the funds for his nephew to travel to America and even a railroad pass for the trip from New York City to upstate New York. It was a way for Friedrich to maintain family ties with the "Old World."

Germans planning to emigrate from the homeland were required to apply for permission to leave.[9] Applicants had to demonstrate that they weren't leaving unpaid debts or dependents behind and they had enough money for the trip. Male applicants had to prove they had served in the military or else be able to convince officials they weren't avoiding conscription, a potential problem for someone like Henry, who was approaching draft age.

In practice, more than half of all emigrants left without bothering to obtain permission from the German government. That's probably because emigrants boarding ships at Bremen needed only to produce a valid steamer ticket and a birth certificate. Henry, however, decided to risk the conscription question and filed a petition to emigrate. It's likely he produced a letter from his uncle inviting him to live in Schenectady. He was one of 516 applicants in the *Kreis Minden* district who obtained approval to emigrate in 1881.[10]

At the same time, Henry booked passage to New York with an agent of the North German Lloyd in Minden. He purchased a ticket in steerage, the part of the ship below decks for passengers who paid the lowest fare, on the *S.S. Donau*, scheduled to sail from Bremerhaven to New York, via Southampton, England, on April 10, 1881. The thirteen-year-old *Donau* was among a fleet of usually profitable ships owned by the North German Lloyd. Although Henry probably didn't know it, the Lloyd had its share of disasters at sea. Six years earlier, the *Deutschland* was lost when the ship ran aground in the English Channel during a fog.[11]

Early in April, Henry bid *auf wiedersehen* (good-bye) to his friends in Hille, many of whom also planned to emigrate. Some, like Christian Thielking, who worked as a hired man for a farmer, would find their way to Schenectady. Another was Louisa, his *Liebste* (sweetheart), and a member of an unrelated Horstmann family in Hille. Two years younger than Henry, Louisa also had relatives who lived in Schenectady. She was one of four children living at #232 with her father. Her mother, Elizabeth (Buttmann) Horstmann, had died three years earlier. No doubt Henry and Louisa talked about their future; she booked passage on the *Donau* later in the year.

Neighbors and friends traditionally held a party in a local inn to send off emigrants like Henry. Many toasts were made to the leave-takers with *Hiller Bast-Korn,* a locally made corn-based spirit, as all sang a farewell: *"Jetzt ist die Zeit und Stunde da, wir fahren ins Amerika* (Now is the time and hour that we journey to America)."

But any merrymaking belied the fact that leaving one's home village was an emotional experience. Leave-taking was so often associated with death that a religious service was held on the eve of departure.[12] It was customary for the pastor of the church to offer prayers for a safe journey. This surely caused Henry to face reality and set aside, at least temporarily, his enthusiasm for the coming trip. Besides his parents, he was leaving five sisters and two brothers. Caroline, at twenty-one the oldest, was planning to marry Carl Husz while Marie, his youngest sister, had just celebrated her first birthday. Three other sisters—Caroline, Sophie, and Frederika—were between three and nine years old. Christian, his older brother, was serving in the army. Friedrich was two years younger than Henry.

Henry's mother, Caroline, held the family together when sickness and death made their too-frequent appearances. She and her husband had buried four children in the Hille churchyard (another would die in 1885). Now she was about to lose another son, this time to America. No doubt she realized that she would never see Henry again—few in the village who left for America ever returned. The journeys were simply too expensive and arduous. *"Gehst du mitt Gott* (God be with you)" were likely the last words she spoke to her departing son.

Although stern and strong-willed, Henry's father was also a compassionate man. Perhaps he wished he had followed his two brothers to America many years before. But the Horstmanns had long been rooted to the same soil, and it was his task to pass it on to the next generation. Even though his son was surely needed on the farm, the elder Horstmann gave him his blessing. Henry would be forever grateful for his father's support.

Henry was not the only villager to book passage on the *S.S. Donau*. According to the ship's manifest, others included the Fegel family— Heinrich, Elisabeth, and their nine-month-old daughter. Twenty-three-year-old August Wehmer, a farm hand, and Wilhelm Brinkmann, a seventeen-year-old from neighboring Eickhorst, were fellow travelers. The two were probably Henry's companions as he traveled by foot north to Bremen, a city by the North Sea some 108 kilometers (sixty-seven miles) distant. For about a week, they followed the Weser River north, finding refuge in villages and on farms as the river wound its way toward the North Sea. They made their way over muddy, rutted roads already crowded with emigrants, some pulling carts piled high with personal possessions.

The emigrants' farewell (a painting by Ludwig
Bokelmann, U.S. Library of Congress)

Arriving in Bremen, a thousand-year-old Hanseatic city,[13] they
wouldn't have missed a colossal statue, "Roland the Giant," that towered
in front of the town hall. As they walked through the city, they steered
clear of the notorious "*bauernfangern*,"[14] con men who preyed upon new
arrivals, especially emigrants. Signs posted throughout the city by the
police warned of the swindlers, pickpockets, and "sharks" who engaged
in unusual businesses like changing money or buying ship tickets.

Once in Bremen their next destination was Bremerhaven, a
port built in the harbor at the mouth of the North Sea and suitably
nicknamed *Der Vorort New-Yorks* (the suburb of New York).[15] It was the
main launching point for the flood of emigrants leaving Germany. To
reach the port they boarded a crude, flat-bottomed vessel known as a

Weser punt. Even though one could get there by rail, the river was the cheapest way to reach Bremerhaven. Bad weather often turned the river journey into a miserable two-day trip. Passengers were required to stay on deck and had no hot food. Once the decrepit vessel approached the docks at Bremerhaven, its passengers could see enormous ships moored in *Neuer Hafen*, the new port.

The iron-hulled *S.S. Donau* dominated the harbor's skyline with its two masts and funnel. Directly behind it stood an immense building, the *"Wartehalle,"* or waiting room, flying the flag of the North German Lloyd Steamship Company. Ships preparing to depart were inspected by Bremen officials to ensure they had adequate provisions, fuel, and lifeboats.

On the docks, passengers were directed to the *"Auswanderunghaus* (emigrant's inn)," a facility built to feed as many as 3,500 travelers and sleep two thousand of them at a time. Food and lodging cost sixty-six pfennig (about a quarter) per night. In the morning passengers gathered their belongings and walked to the *Wartehalle* where they were examined by a doctor (German law required each emigrant to have a medical exam before embarking). A doctor asked simply, "Are you in good health? Put out your tongue!" Each traveler was issued tinware and a straw mattress. The mattress, they were told, should be thrown overboard at the end of their journey.[16]

Exiting onto the pier, Henry and his companions boarded the awesome ship via a steep ladder to the main deck, clutching their bags of personal belongings. Other passengers held on to young children and waved tearful farewells to family and friends on the pier below. A din of voices swept over the pier like a breaking wave in the languages and dialects of Saxony, Thuringia, Bavaria, Hungary, and Austria. Many emigrants were destined for cities in America with names like Cincinnati, Milwaukee, and St. Louis. Others planned to meet relatives in New York City's *Kleindeutschland* (little Germany), the largest German-speaking community outside of Germany.[17]

Dispatch hall of the North German Lloyd in
Bremerhaven in 1870 (Source: Wikipedia)

At the top of the gangway, the ship's purser inspected identification
papers and tickets. Henry presented his birth certificate and ticket for
passage in steerage. The purser entered his name on the ship's manifest:
Heinr. Horstmann, 17, m, workman, Prussia, U.S.A., Steerage.[18]

Like any youngster leaving home for the first time, Henry must
have been overwhelmed with conflicting emotions. Aboard the gigantic,
smelly ship teeming with people who spoke in strange tongues, he had
ample reason to question whether he was making the right decision. His
excitement was checked by the realization he was leaving the safety of
his family and village, probably never to see them again. Now he had
to cross an ocean he had never seen to reach a place he could barely
imagine. Once the ship got underway there was no turning back.

Three

ATLANTIC CROSSING

*First and second class and steerage passengers live apart, each class in
its own part of the great steamer. But if one could cast the horoscope of
each passenger, what strange and startling changes might be foretold!*

Harper's Weekly, November 7, 1874

On the morning of April 10, 1881, the *S.S. Donau* prepared to
depart from its berth at Bremerhaven. Built for *Norddeutscher
Lloyd*, the 332-foot long steamer had a 40-foot beam, a clipper bow, two
masts, and one funnel. Below decks was a 600 horsepower engine that
powered the single-screw vessel at a service speed of 13 knots. She was
designed to accommodate 60 first class and 700 third class passengers,
along with a crew of 90–105.[1]

The three thousand-ton, iron-hulled steamship was an improved
version of earlier wooden-hulled sailing ships that had brought Henry's
two uncles, Friedrich and Carl Horstmann, to America. Henry had
surely heard stories about his uncles' earlier passage across the Atlantic
but the frightful tales didn't deter him from his decision. The voyage
from Bremen to New York in the 1850s averaged about six weeks
during which an estimated one out of every six passengers died or
became dangerously ill at sea. Passengers on the sailing vessels faced
illnesses like seasickness, diarrhea, constipation, scurvy, ulcers, and

trench mouth. As if that weren't enough, 6 percent of all German ships departing Bremen arrived in North America with cases of cholera on board.[2]

Six weeks at sea also increased the danger of encountering a storm. When this happened, steerage passengers were tossed about like marbles as they screamed and prayed for calm waters. "A sudden heave of the ship," observed a congressional committee investigating the immigrant trade, "often dislodged whole families from their berths and hurled them headlong among their companions who lay on the opposite side."[3] When all was calm at sea, steerage passengers were required to work in the galley, swab the gangways, empty chamber pots, and wash clothes. No one was allowed to remain in his bunk, no matter how sick, unless the ship was in stormy weather. Fortunately for Henry, the *S.S. Donau* was capable of spanning the Atlantic in as little as ten days—provided the ship's captain correctly guessed the weather conditions. Although a steamship, her two sailing masts could be deployed in case of a propeller or engine failure.

The passengers' welfare was not the highest priority for the *Donau*'s captain, Richard Brussius. Like most captains in the emigrant trade, his main objective was to make as many runs across the Atlantic as he could while the weather was cooperative. The emigrant trade was a profitable business for shipping companies like the North German Lloyd and the Hamburg-America line. They competed fiercely with each other for the booming passenger traffic generated by the mass exodus of people fleeing from their European homelands.

Transatlantic steamship captains were much-admired figures of their day. Those who commanded the North German Lloyd ships were reportedly "the peers of any men who sailed the sea" and were highly regarded for their "seamanship and social qualities," according to an 1886 profile of sea-going captains. Richard Brussius, described as a "universally popular" commander, completed more than one hundred round trip voyages across the Atlantic. "He takes pains to see that all who cross with him are comfortable and happy," the review noted, adding that "he has a good voice, is fond of music, and is brimful of anecdotes..."[4]

As the *Donau* made its way into the North Sea, Henry glimpsed continental Europe for the last time. How much he could see was dependent upon the weather; rain and fog were more likely than sunshine in this region of northern Europe. The diked lowlands of the Netherlands, sparsely dotted with thatched farmhouses and windmills, were typical of his *Heimat* (homeland). They were vistas that he would never see again.

The emigrant ship steamed south through the narrow Straits of Dover as passengers on deck marveled at the sight of majestic chalk-white cliffs towering over the south coast of England. Entering the English Channel, the *Donau* made a brief stop at Southampton to pick up a few English passengers. Later, when the clipper-bowed vessel took its first wallow into the hulking waves of the Atlantic Ocean, the youthful emigrant would discover the full meaning of *Seekrankenheit*, the German expression for seasickness.

Passengers assigned to the steerage area below decks used their own straw mattresses and eating utensils for the journey. There was no dining room; they had to eat on tables between isles that separated rows of two-foot-wide berths. Under German law, food was free on all ships departing from Bremerhaven. But most of it was inedible even if one was not seasick. A typical complaint was that the salt pork was hard and tasteless, the salt fish so bad it was thrown overboard, and the oatmeal black and full of beetles.[5]

Crowded quarters afforded little privacy. Poor ventilation contributed to seasickness and could spread illnesses from those who carried diseases. The claustrophobic space and foul air forced steerage passengers up to the main deck for fresh air and sunshine. On some ships, crew members had scant regard for the emigrants' basic needs and were known to take advantage of unwitting ones, especially women.

Like Henry, nearly all of the steerage passengers were seeing an ocean for the first time. Some believed the Atlantic was nothing more than a wide river. But most knew that the journey was not without risk—the prospect of shipwreck or fire surely preyed on their minds. Stories of disasters at sea were widely known and circulated among the immigrants. Eight years earlier, the British steamship *Atlantic*, a somewhat larger ship than the *Donau*, was carrying 862 people, mostly emigrants, from Liverpool to New York when it was caught in mid-ocean by heavy gales. The ship made a run for the nearest port in Halifax, Nova Scotia, but ran onto rocks and broke up. It was one of the worst calamities ever at sea to that point—546 passengers and crew members lost their lives.[6] (The *Donau* itself would be destroyed after catching fire in the North Atlantic and sinking in March 1895.[7])

No first-person account of the *Donau's* April 1881 ocean crossing is known to exist so it is not possible to verify whether Captain Brussius lived up to his plaudits. But a sense of what a typical journey on an emigrant steamship was like can be gleaned from the words of sixteen-year-old Wilhelm Bürkert, who departed from Hamburg five years earlier on another ship. He wrote this letter to his family after he disembarked in New York: [8]

> *Praise be to the Lord…for you can count yourself lucky to have arrived here safely, especially when you hear that at the same time our ship left, on the same water, no less than 3 ships sank from running into one another in the fog.*
>
> *I was all the way in front in the first group of berths. I had to eat with 11 others, and carve the meat. Every day…meat, potatoes and rice soup, except for the 2 Sundays, when we had pudding along with it. Oh, I believe that stuff was boiled in sea water, it made me so sick. I ate nothing and drank nothing.*
>
> *The next morning everyone was already seasick. For on the open sea, the ship rolls terribly. It goes as fast as an express train… out on the Atlantic Ocean the ship really started to roll and the waves went clear up to the helmsman.*
>
> *I and 2 other friends…did not get seasick. Everybody was on top deck. One person puked here, another over there, for in steerage, way down at the bottom, you couldn't stand it.*
>
> *The last few days we had such a storm that you couldn't stand up or lie down. The trunks we had with us were tied down. The*

last night we had fog…At 4 in the morning we heard land-land. And that is a sight, oh splendid.

Here the anchor was cast. A doctor came out about 7 o'clock and examined each one to see if he had a contagious disease. Everyone was healthy…Here we had to go on a small ship…At 3 o'clock in the afternoon we arrived in New-York.

Here we all went into a garden where a speech was held. It was Castle Garden, which is set up to take care of emigrants.

Although few details are known about the *Donau's* voyage, a day-after report in the *New York Times* observed that the ship encountered an iceberg "of considerable height" along the coast of Newfoundland.[9] That looming mountain of ice in the midst of a seemingly unending sea was surely an otherworldly sight to the ship's astonished passengers.

The months from March through July are witness to shimmering ice giants that break off from huge glaciers in West Greenland and make their way into the coastal waters of Newfoundland. The scenario aboard a ship when a forward lookout shouts "Ice—dead ahead!" is chilling.

A hair-raising account of such an encounter was reported from a ship crossing the Atlantic not long after the *Donau:* "For an instant then, they (passengers) hear the sound of sea breaking as upon an iron coast. A tall shadow appears in the mist, the dim outline of peaks and spires. Shout follows shout from the lookouts by the bow; the fog splits asunder as an over-towering cliff appears—a cathedral of ice, a heavy base rising to pinnacles, all of the deepest blue. Harshly, the waves ply apart its flanks, and a great tremor falls upon the ship, quivering fore and aft under the strokes of its screws. Then she draws from the impending doom, slips by so close that one may peer into the caves and valleys of the berg.…The ship veers off, her whistle blowing in terror. Her helm is turned, she points upward on her course, and at three-quarters speed, again goes driving on her way.[10]

On April 22, 1881, twelve days after departing from Bremerhaven, the *S.S. Donau* made its way into New York harbor trailed by seagulls shrieking their welcome. No doubt it was an electrifying sight for Henry and the ship's passengers as New York City emerged from the fog at daybreak to reveal a spectacular scene of factories, churches, tenements, and public buildings. The harbor was bustling, teeming with boats of all shapes and sizes carrying people and goods, many riding low in the water with cargoes of coal and wheat. There was no Statue of Liberty to greet the tired, poor, and huddled masses—she would make her first appearance in the harbor eleven years later. And hidden from the passengers' view were thousands of men, women, and children—many of them immigrants—who toiled in the city's notorious sweatshops.

Weary passengers cheered as the *Donau* fired a salute and anchored in sight of a circular, castlelike building with brown stone walls near the Battery at the southern tip of Manhattan. Two barges pushed by tugboats pulled alongside the immigrant ship. Baggage was placed in one while passengers boarded the other. With help from the tugs, the barges carefully threaded their way through the boat traffic cluttering the harbor to a landing pier. At the landing, Captain Brussius presented his handwritten manifest to waiting U.S. Customs officials.

The following day a *New York Times* column headed "Marine Intelligence" announced the arrival of the steamship *Donau* with "merchandise and passengers" from Bremen, Germany and Southampton, England. From the newspaper's brief account, a casual reader could easily conclude that the vessel was a freighter carrying only a few passengers.[11] But in fact, the *S. S. Donau's* manifest filed with the Port of New York on April 22, 1881 listed a total of 959 passengers. Crammed between decks with Henry in steerage were 463 adults and 153 children (33 of them infants).[12] The thirteen-year-old steamship was 199 passengers over its official limit and in violation of German and American seaworthiness laws. No doubt Henry and his fellow travelers were unaware of this transgression; they were simply relieved to have finally reached *terra firma* in America.

Six ships disgorged nearly four thousand immigrants in New York City that day, most of them German, Irish, and Italian. The *Times* reported that eight more ships due to arrive by week's end would raise the total number of immigrant arrivals to more than twenty thousand—the greatest number ever recorded by the city in one week's time.[13]

By the end of the year, more than 200,000 German immigrants had arrived in the United States—the second-highest total ever recorded in a single year. And by the end of the decade, a million and a half had fled the German Empire for America, more than any other decade before or since.[14]

The immigrants' arrival seemed to confirm Herman Melville's observation: "If they can get here, they have God's right to come."[15] One of them, Henry Horstmann, was a tall, seventeen-year-old, self-described "workman" from Prussia carrying his worldly possessions in a travel bag. Besides his birth certificate and a train ticket to upstate New York, he carried an unshakeable determination to become a *lokomotivfuhrer.*

Henry came to America on the S.S. Donau, a North German Lloyd steamship out of Bremen, in 1881. Four months later, his future wife, Louisa, made the crossing on the same ship. The iron-clad vessel was built to accommodate 760 passengers. (Courtesy of The Mariners' Museum, Newport News, Virginia)

Four

A Place Called Hell

*A place of unlawful detention, a place for tyranny and
whimsical rule … a place for the disgrace of the nation
in the eyes of those who desire to become citizens.*

The *New York World*, 1887[1]

Henry and his fellow travelers had landed at Castle Garden, a place
described by another newspaper as "a curious hybrid between a
fortress and a prison of the last century. The interior is gloom, dirt, decay
and hideousness … the rotunda, corridors, and rooms are cold, poorly
lighted, badly ventilated, foul smelling and repulsive … In reality, it is
a disgrace to the Empire State and the Federal government."[2]

Originally a fort built at the southern tip of Manhattan, the aging
structure once served as an entertainment center where Jenny Lind, the
"Swedish Nightingale," crooned before sell-out audiences. The structure
was converted to the nation's first Emigrant Landing Depot in 1855
upon reports that unsuspecting immigrants left off by their ships at
the city's wharf were being fleeced by thugs and thieves as they sought
housing, food, and railway tickets.[3] The idea was that Castle Garden
would provide protection for arriving immigrants and allow the U.S.
Government to record their names, nationalities, and destinations while
deciding which ones were likely to become public charges, i.e., those

who were blind, crippled, or otherwise disabled. A twelve-foot-high fence around the building was designed to keep the swindlers out.

At the time of Henry's arrival, the decrepit Castle Garden was hardly a welcoming center. Worse yet, corruption was rampant. A federal investigation concluded that administration of the facility was "a perfect farce."[4] Clerks of the Emigration Commission bullied immigrants while railroad agents and money changers gouged them. The *New York World* reported wholesale robbery of immigrants at Castle Garden. Contingents of con men, swindlers, and prostitutes plied their trades just outside the fence that encircled the building. "Runners" steered new arrivals to overpriced, run-down lodgings. Baggage handlers demanded "*trinkgelt* (drinking money)" if the newcomers hoped to see their belongings again. One agent told investigators: "We call Castle Garden Hell, and don't expect to change Hell."[5]

Once cleared by Customs officials and doctors who weeded out the sick and destitute, the *Donau's* weary passengers were directed through a dungeonlike door set in a red sandstone archway and up a musty corridor into the interior of the building. There, the sight of thousands of people milling in the rotunda was an astonishing contrast to the twelve days and nights they had spent at sea with nothing to watch but seagulls, churning water, and an occasional passing ship.

The rotunda, a huge area that held up to four thousand people, swarmed with people garbed in the traditional garments of their homelands—Swedish and Bohemian peasants, Hungarian miners in flaring hats and sheepskin coats, Russian Jews, and Arabs in fez and scarlet trousers. Henry and other immigrants from German-speaking lands wore long-skirted, dark blue woolen coats and flat military caps. Customs officials treated the German-speakers relatively well because they obeyed instructions and helped each other along.

An open timber roof spanned the enclosure of the massive old walls. A section of wooden seats surrounded by board fences divided the interior into something resembling holding pens for cattle. There was no bath or private washroom for cleaning up after twelve days in steerage, just a few stationary basins. Only one restaurant was on the premise, a lunch counter that served up cheap sausage, coarse bread, and a mystery coffee. It was cheap but probably tasted a lot better than the food on their ship. Many immigrants prepared their own meals on the iron cooking stoves placed throughout the rotunda. Those tired and worn out from seasickness had to make beds out of the wooden seats or sleep on the dirty floor. It was a scenario made to order for a popular song: "Nobody cares for my grief or distress/Friendless am I in the new world today," ran the lyrics from the ballad "Only An Emigrant."[6]

Loud calls announced the names of relatives and friends who had come to meet new arrivals. Clerks stood by at desks to write letters and send telegrams in most European languages. Missionaries circulated in the crowd to give advice and distribute religious books.

One by one, the apprehensive travelers were checked out by an officer of the Emigration Commission and a translator who questioned them in their native languages. U.S. immigration law at the time excluded prostitutes and persons who had been sentenced to jail in their homelands. The new arrivals had to prove their identities and confirm they had relatives or friends who would take them in. Henry's birth certificate and his railroad pass no doubt helped him pass these hurdles (he may also have carried a letter from his uncle Friedrich).

A German-speaking officer mounted a rostrum and addressed the *Donau*'s passengers. Those not prepared to pay for a place to stay could sleep inside the building. He pointed out where they could get information about railway tickets and jobs and change their money.

The first stop was at the desk of a so-called "booker," a clerk of the Railway Association, whose duty was to determine where the passenger was going and to issue a printed slip indicating the ticket price. Here Henry could ask, "*Wann geht der nachste Zug nach Schenectady* (When is the next train to Schenectady)?" Other travelers were directed to the railway counter, where a ticket could be purchased. Corrupt bookers worked with ticket agents to inflate prices. New arrivals who had no money to pay for further transportation had no choice but to remain in the city. Henry was one of the fortunate ones who had arrived with a rail ticket in hand.

Money merchants posted their rates for exchanging foreign and domestic money on blackboards. The constantly changing rates caused great confusion, giving the brokers an open invitation to defraud unsuspecting immigrants. Exclamations of *"Das kann ich nicht verstehen* (I don't understand)" were frequent, but there was no choice other than to accept the broker's word.

Outside of Castle Garden, "runners" eagerly awaited the new arrivals. They were ready to con them out of their possessions, sell them overpriced railroad tickets, or lure them to boarding houses where owners would swindle them out of their meager resources. Employers looking to hire immigrants posted jobs on a blackboard in German and other languages.

The New York German Society, headed by Friedrich Kapp, a prominent German-American author and lawyer, was on hand to protect and assist the new arrivals. German-speaking emissaries passed out city maps, warning newcomers to stay away from Washington

Interior of Rotunda at Castle Garden (*Harpers New Monthly Magazine,* March 1871*).*

Street where thieves waited for those who dared venture into that unsavory part of the city. In fact, New York was a sinkhole of crime. Crammed into fetid tenements, thousands of city dwellers, native born and immigrants alike, depended on crime for their survival. Youths known as "street rats" or "guttersnipes," lived, slept, and ate in the city streets and alleys. Pickpockets were everywhere and newly arrived immigrants were their prime targets.

How could a seventeen-year-old farm boy who couldn't speak English and had never been in a city anywhere near the size of New York find his way from the Battery to the Grand Central Depot? Nothing in Henry's experience had prepared him for the sights and smells of a city of 1.2 million residents jammed into tenements that housed more than sixteen persons per dwelling. The streets of lower Manhattan, clogged with horse-drawn carriages and pedestrians, overflowed with "spectacular accumulations" of garbage mostly generated by horses that daily produced an estimated four hundred tons of manure, twenty thousand gallons of urine, and almost two hundred carcasses. Trash, dirt, and filth were piled high in gutters, sometimes reaching knee level—a tribute to corruption in the city's garbage removal system.[7]

With proper directions, Henry might have taken a train from Battery Park to Grand Central Depot. To do so, he could have taken the Third Avenue elevated system (the El) from its South Ferry station, or a Second Avenue line that ran north from Chatham Square. It would have been a spectacular ride for the newcomer as the El raced above the four- and five-story tenement buildings below.[8] If he chose not to ride the El, another option was the horse car, a taxilike service provided by thirty-two rival street lines, many of which ran directly beneath the El. Although the cheapest way to travel other than walking, the horse cars were poorly ventilated, their straw-strewn floors full of vermin, and their drivers exhausted from sixteen-hour days of work at miserly wages.

With little, if any, money to spare, it's more than likely that Henry walked the nearly four miles from the Battery to the Grand Central Depot at Forty-Second Street and Fourth Avenue. Following Broadway north past City Hall Park, he would find himself on the outskirts of Kleindeutschland, a German-speaking community on the lower East Side that included *Plattdeutsche*, Hessians, Bavarians, and Prussians. Here he could at least speak with people who could give him directions. The city counted 163,482 German-born residents in 1880 (only two cities in the world had more Germans, Berlin and Vienna).[9]

Reaching Union Square, Henry couldn't miss the so-called "sun towers," 160-foot masts topped with clusters of arc lights that bathed Broadway in brilliant light at nighttime.[10] And at Madison Square, high above the trees loomed a huge thirty-two-foot, metal-sheathed arm holding a lighted torch. Seated on a pedestal, the arm itself was taller than "Roland the Giant" in Bremen. The strange object was an appendage of the yet-to-be assembled Statue of Liberty, a gift from France, which would greet future immigrants as they arrived in New York harbor.[11]

At Broadway and Fifth Avenue, horse-drawn delivery trucks loaded with barrels and crates clogged the roadways as they tried to bull their way across the busy intersection. Pedestrians were assaulted by the deafening noise of clopping horses and ironclad wagon wheels clanging on the cobblestones amid the shouts and curses of drivers.

Fifth Avenue presented an entirely different view of the city. Hotels, shops, and fancy residences must have dazzled the eyes of the German farm boy. One brownstone building nearing completion at 640 Fifth Avenue was an incredible block-long four-story mansion with a grand hall at its center that reached to the roof. When completed in the fall, its bronze entrance doors, called "the Gates of Paradise," depicted scenes of Heaven from the Old Testament.[12] The owner of this lavish, palacelike residence was William H. Vanderbilt, widely known to the public as a "robber baron."

The sight that greeted Henry when he finally reached his destination at cobblestoned Forty-Second Street and Fourth Avenue was stunning. The Grand Central Depot, a stupendous red brick structure that dominated the city's skyline, was the crown jewel of William H. Vanderbilt's New York Central and Hudson River Railroad. One hundred feet tall at its highest point, the Depot covered five full acres of city ground. The cast-iron trimmings on its walls were painted white to look like marble. Sections of glass ran along a domed roof supported by elaborate iron trusses and topped off with five turrets. An L-shaped building at the side contained ticket offices and waiting rooms enclosed in an enormous glass arched roof. Vanderbilt boasted that it was the most magnificent railroad station in the world.[13]

On or about April 23, 1881, Henry boarded a New York Central train at the Grand Central Depot packed with fellow immigrants traveling to cities in New York State like Albany, Schenectady, Rochester, and Buffalo. Some were even headed beyond Buffalo and the Great Lakes to search for fertile farmland in the Midwest. Excited but travel-weary, Henry knew nothing of William H. Vanderbilt, owner of the railroad that was to influence the course of his future in America.

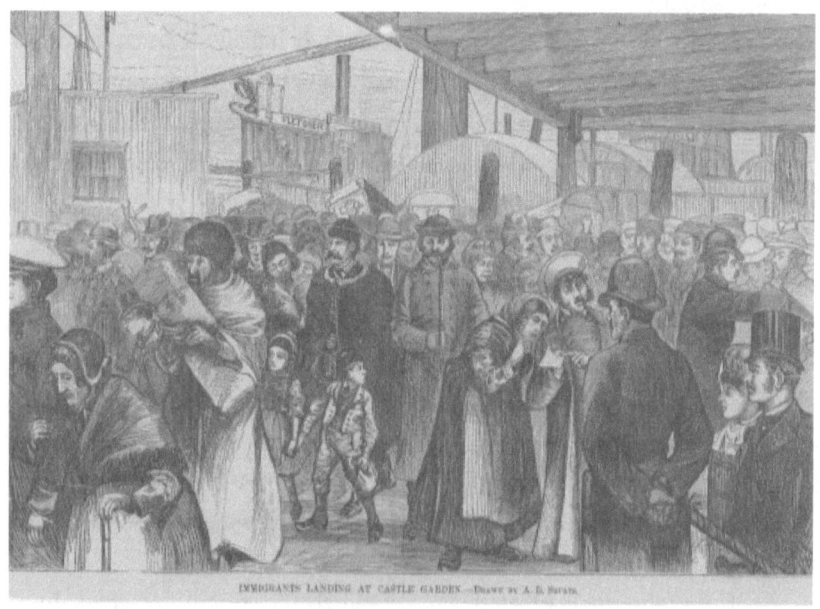

Immigrants Landing at Castle Garden (Harper's Weekly, 1880)

Five

TRANSFORMATION

*What he brings is strength and energy, and the will and capacity to
work is far more potent, because it is more enduring, and because it
is continued and multiplied in his children and in their children.*

Harper's Weekly, June 11, 1881

Engineer Friedrich Horstmann must have wondered how he would
recognize his nephew as he waited for a New York Central train
at the Schenectady Depot one day in April 1881. No doubt, the scene
rekindled his memory of nearly thirty years before when he, too, was
an anxious teenage immigrant who spoke only *Platt Deutsch*.

But there could be no mistaking the young man who stepped
off the train amid the throng of immigrants carrying valises, packs,
bags, and trunks of all sizes. The tall, slender youth with deep-set blue
eyes and an aquiline nose had an uncanny resemblance to Friedrich's
brother in Hille.

Separation from their homeland was a painful experience for many
immigrants away from their homes and villages for the first time,
facing strange new customs and a language they didn't understand.
But Henry had followed others from his village to an American city
with an established, close-knit German community. About 10 percent
of Schenectady's population, about three thousand residents, were

German-born.[1] Many of them were emigrants from *Kreis Minden*, the district in Westphalia that encompassed Hille and other villages. Henry recognized familiar Hille names like Brandhorst, Grannemann, Lukens, Rothemeier, Gerding, von Behren, Wege, Thuener, and Whitmyer. Even Henry's surname was a common one—besides his two uncles, five unrelated Horstmann men worked and lived in the city, including William Horstmann, a "hostler" who serviced locomotives. These were people who spoke his language and knew what it was like to arrive as a "greenhorn" from the Old Country.

Friedrich Horstmann's house at 80 Liberty Street near the train depot was bursting at the seams. He and his wife Caroline (nee Pepper) had eight children, and she was pregnant with another. Because they had no room for Henry, Friedrich took his nephew across the Mohawk River to Glenville, a town just north of the Mohawk River where his brother, Carl Ludwig Horstmann, was farming.

Carl and his wife Caroline (nee Schumacher) also had a large and growing family, numbering five children at the time. Settling first in Rexford, by 1880 they had saved enough money to buy three hundred acres of farmland in Glenville. Although their farm had a full complement of farmhands and couldn't accommodate another, Charles knew a neighboring farmer who was in need of help.

The farm's owner at the time, an elderly man named Cramer, was confined to a wheelchair as the result of a run-in he had had with a bull. His son-in-law, John McMichael, ran the farm (it later became known by his name) and an adjoining broom-making factory. Finding good labor was difficult; McMichael had to travel to Albany to hire day laborers.

Broomcorn supported a thriving industry in the Schenectady area—broom-making factories were located on both sides of the Mohawk River, which divided the countryside from the city. The crop grew along the flat lands on both sides of the Mohawk, much as it did along the Weser River near Hille in Germany. Planted and harvested by hand, broomcorn grew up to fifteen feet tall and produced bushes of stiff fibers that were fashioned into brooms and brushes. Raising, harvesting, and turning broomcorn into brooms provided jobs for many of Glenville's 2,700 residents.

Henry was exactly the sort of help John McMichael needed—a hardworking German lad willing to work in return for room and board plus $1.00 a day. McMichael's mother-in-law, herself a German immigrant, would teach him English. He could be trained to operate machinery as he shared quarters with other hired hands in a bunkhouse adjacent to the broom-making factory.

Not long after Henry settled into life on the McMichael farm, his sixteen-year-old sweetheart, Louisa Horstmann, landed at Castle Garden and made her way to Schenectady. Henry had likely written her with details about his trip and his job, encouraging her to make the journey. She, too, crossed the Atlantic on the *S.S. Donau*, arriving in New York on August 26, 1881,[2] with a wooden trunk containing her possessions, among them her bible, *die Heilige Schrift*. She was traveling with Hille villagers Caroline Fegel, Caroline Brockmeyer, and Heinrich Lange.

Like Henry, Louisa had suffered the loss of many family members in Hille. Besides her mother, she had lost a sister to a mysterious illness. Louisa arrived in America on the day her father remarried in Hille, perhaps an indication she wasn't pleased with his remarriage. Later, her sister Marie and two brothers (Friedrich and Heinrich), all born at Hille #232, followed her to Schenectady.

Louisa also had two uncles living in Schenectady, Charles (C.F.) and Christian Horstmann who had emigrated from Hille about a decade earlier. They ran a company in Schenectady that produced brooms and whisk brushes. When it failed, Charles became a silk merchant and Christian opened a tailor shop. She had other Horstmann relatives, too—cousins in Glenville and in nearby Amsterdam.

Henry worked dawn to dusk on the McMichael farm during planting and harvesting, often seven days a week. In the spring, broomcorn seed was planted by hand with a wheel planter. At harvest time, field hands cut the broomcorn stalks, loaded them onto wagons, and took them to the broom shop where they were laid out on slats to dry. Once dry, the stalks were secured onto handles and made into brooms and brushes in the factory, where another machine flattened and sewed the brush. The factory produced round brooms called hurl or hearth brooms and flat ones called Shaker brooms that sold for a dollar a dozen.[3]

Cramer-McMichael house on farm where Henry worked.

Field hands cutting broomcorn. Tall worker (third from left) may be Henry. (Photos courtesy of Schenectady County Historical Society.)

The McMichael farm provided easy access to Schenectady, where Henry could visit Louisa and his Uncle Friedrich. It was a short trip by horse or wagon from Glenville into the city across the Iron Bridge over the Mohawk River. Schenectady boasted cobblestone pavements, gas and oil lamps, hitching posts for horses, and wood-covered street cisterns. Horse cars lurched their way along State Street, a main thoroughfare lined with hotels and shops, including the Givens Hotel, a popular eating place and rooming house. Not long after Henry's arrival, shops and stores in the city were draped in black and white in mourning for President James Garfield, assassinated at a railroad station in the nation's capital.

Henry and Louisa's relationship blossomed as they adapted to their new lives. In the summer they could walk to Crescent Park where band concerts were held and herb doctors like Big Jim Cuff, a six-foot, seven-inch descendent of Mohawk Indians, put on medicine shows. Parades and a one-ring circus with a Wild West show were always attractions, as were balloon ascensions that drew big crowds. Some couples would go for a Sunday afternoon ride in a closed-coupe coach pulled by a team of horses from Hathaway's Livery.

They could skate on the Erie Canal in the frigid upstate New York winter where temperatures sometimes dropped as low as twenty-eight degrees below zero. The canal, sometimes called "Clinton's Ditch" (after an early New York Governor), was a man-made waterway that ran directly through the city as it crossed the state between Albany and Buffalo. The arcticlike winters also brought "bobbing" contests, races between bobsled teams on wooden sleds that streaked down a steep and icy hill on Union Street.[4]

The city's German Methodist Church had many members born in Henry and Louisa's *Heimat* (hometown). The church dated back to the early part of the century when a little colony of *Kirchendeutsch,* or "church Germans," migrated from Hille to "Old Dorp," as Schenectady was then known. Early settlers named von Behren, Kasten, Dannenburg, and Pepper had to travel by wagon to Albany to attend church services until a pastor was dispatched from New York City. As German immigrants poured into the city, the church grew into one of the largest German-speaking Methodist congregations in the United States. A new building was erected in 1872 at the corner of Lafayette and Union Streets.[5] Church records show that Henry became a member of the congregation in 1887 when Reverend F.H. Rey was its pastor.[6]

During his time on the McMichael farm, Henry learned to speak and read English. He also displayed a talent for working with machinery in the broom-making factory, a skill which likely caught the eye of his uncle Friedrich.

Friedrich Horstmann had only one son, Charles, who was bent on becoming a druggist and showed no interest in railroading. Henry, on the other hand, was clearly determined to follow in his uncle's footsteps as an engineer. So it was natural for Friedrich to take his young nephew under his wing and expose him to a trainman's work. As a Central engineer, Friedrich had access to the "Big Shop" in Schenectady, a massive factory where several thousand laborers built and repaired locomotives. It was an ideal place to educate a potential railroader.

Officially known as the Schenectady Locomotive Works, the Big Shop was widely known for its high quality, fast-running engines produced under the direction of Walter McQueen, an ingenious master mechanic considered one of the greatest steam-locomotive builders of all time. His most famous engine was the Jupiter, built for the Central Pacific Railroad, which linked up with a Union Pacific locomotive at Promontory, Utah to mark completion of the Transcontinental Railroad on May 10, 1869.[7]

By the '80s, the Big Shop was turning out heavy American-type 4-4-0 locomotives ("4-4-0" designates four pilot wheels, four driving wheels, and no trailing wheels). Locomotives were built from start to finish in the factory. Metal frames for the engines were constructed in the machine shop, cylinders and wheels in the foundry, and boilers in the boiler shop. In the erecting shop, the engine's parts were assembled and a crane lifted the locomotive and slid pairs of wheels into place. The engine's cab was assembled separately and put in place with its controls intact. Finally, in the livery, the engine's cab was painted with colors requested by its railroad customer, and the locomotive was ready for testing.[8]

LOCOMOTIVES OF STANDARD DESIGN FOR ALL CLASSES OF SERVICE,
OR FROM DESIGNS FURNISHED BY RAILROAD COMPANIES.

But the place that grabbed Henry's attention more than any other was the New York Central's West Albany Yard, an enormous 350-acre complex that was a staging point for the Central's trains. It was a place where Friedrich could show his nephew what was involved in running and maintaining an iron horse. The massive facility was one of the largest servicing terminals on the Central's system. Crews labored there day and night fueling, watering, servicing, and repairing trains destined for all points on the Central's expanding system. Its shops repaired an estimated sixty to seventy thousand freight cars every year.[9]

It was an incredibly noisy workplace where one's ears were assaulted by constantly blaring engine bells and whistles, clanking couplers, and a never-ending rumble of rolling wheels. In the engine house, men loaded goods into freight cars and readied passenger and freight trains for service. The railroad never slept or took a holiday; trains arrived at all hours of day and night.

Engineer Horstmann got his daily assignments from the stationmaster at the West Albany Yard. Senior "Eagle-Eyes" like Friedrich were assigned to specific locomotives and took great personal pride in keeping their engines in top-notch condition. Enginemen arriving to get their assignments traded information about conditions on the line as they picked up their train orders at the "beehive," the stationmaster's office. Freight trains with questionable schedules earned the nickname "Maybe"—*Maybe* we'll get there in time to start back on schedule, or *Maybe* we won't.[10]

From the right side of the cab the engineer operated an imposing array of more than fifty controls, each serving a specific purpose. A steam locomotive could travel about one hundred miles before it needed to be refueled and lubricated, dump its ashes, and pick up sand for braking. Once in the cab, some engineers would say a quiet prayer for the job ahead. They knew the unexpected could happen at any time; a single miscalculation, missed signal, or mechanical failure could be disastrous. Working for the Central or any railroad was not for the fainthearted. There was no limit on the number of hours that the men who ran the trains were required to work. Weather, too, could be a crucial factor on any run. And working on a train in the middle of a New York state winter was not for everyone. Injuries and deaths were recurring facts of life on the rails. This was underscored by a tragic accident on January 13, 1882, when the Central's *Atlantic Express*, bound from Albany to New York, stopped to repair its brakes just before a steep curve at Spuyten Duyvil, a village on the Hudson River. As workmen struggled, a local train from Tarrytown running at full speed crashed into it, setting two rear parlor cars on fire. Passengers jammed between the seats were unable to escape the fire as it swept through the fast-burning wooden cars. Ten passengers died in the accident while numerous others were seriously injured. A New York state senator, Webster Wagner, founder of a company that built sleeping cars for the Central, was among the dead.

The crash and resulting fire consumed two of the train's thirteen cars, one named the *Vanderbilt*. The railroad blamed the disaster on a flagman who allegedly failed to warn the approaching train. Then it shifted blame to the engineman of the Tarrytown train who, it claimed, was not sufficiently vigilant. But *Harper's Weekly* charged that a proper system of signaling would have prevented the accident. Lives were "sacrificed to the parsimony of a great and wealthy corporation," the newspaper reported. The train, the newspaper alleged, would not have caught fire "but for the wretched and criminal parsimony of the company in heating the cars with stoves."[11]

The calamity at Spuyten Duyvil and the Central's attempt to lay the blame on its workers betrayed a cavalier attitude that accidents were first and foremost a "human problem" caused by careless workers. The railroad claimed its workers knew the risks of railroading and it was up to them to fend for themselves.

Friedrich Horstmann was well versed in the New York Central's history. The railroad veteran worked for the Central twelve years before Commodore Vanderbilt seized control of the railroad in 1867. He was an engineer in the Utica & Schenectady Division of the Central, a railroad formed by an earlier merger of ten local lines that stretched across New York State between Albany and Niagara Falls. When Vanderbilt took control of the New York Central, the empire-building tycoon combined it with his Hudson River Railroad, renaming the company accordingly.[12] Vanderbilt then declared the new company was worth $45 million more than the railroads were worth separately and proceeded to issue $45 million in new stock for himself. Some on Wall Street called it the greatest job of "stock watering" ever accomplished in America.[13]

Although Commodore Vanderbilt was dead by the time Henry arrived in America, stories about the shipping and railroad magnate were legendary. The egocentric tycoon was poorly educated but a fierce competitor who didn't shy away from manipulating stock and bribing public officials. A nineteenth-century Donald Trump, the crusty Commodore once proposed a 625-foot-high monument to commemorate his achievements—together with those of George Washington—in New York City's Central Park.[14] He later scaled down the monument's size and scope (it was larger than the Washington Monument) and ordered a garish bronze sculpture atop the St. John's Park freight terminal, a work of art described by one critic as "bestial."[15]

William H. Vanderbilt, the Commodore's son, inherited the bulk of his father's estate, including controlling interest in the New York Central. His share was valued at $95 million—an incredible sum for the time, equal to the total amount of funds held by the United States Treasury.[16] Although "Billy" held high-level jobs with the Central, the question of the day was whether he was up to the task of running his father's transport empire. The answer soon became clear.

Within months of his father's death in 1877, William H. Vanderbilt and other railroad chieftains were faced with a strike by railroad workers protesting wage cuts. Violence broke out in many cities. In Pittsburgh, the destruction was compared to the burning of Atlanta in the Civil War.[17] When the strike reached the Central, Vanderbilt simply ignored the strikers while Friedrich Horstmann's union, the Brotherhood of Locomotive Engineers (BLE), the oldest and most powerful union of railroad workers, declared that its members would run the trains no matter what other workers did.

Within a week, the strike against the Central collapsed. Vanderbilt's wage cuts held, but he announced he would donate $100,000 to the Central's loyal employees, to be divided as they saw fit. Loyal engineers got $30 in cash, passenger conductors $20, and brakemen $9. Vanderbilt's actions, coupled with his subsequent rescinding of the wage cut, were calculated to make it appear that he actually cared about his rank-and-file workers.

The Vanderbilt family and its railroads were among the most powerful political forces in New York State, if not the entire country. As one newspaper in England put it: "In some essential ways the family holds the trade of New York in the hollow of their hands, and no business worth the name can be started anywhere along the railways they command without their support and sanction."[18]

With all that power, Vanderbilt and the New York Central were not popular with the public. They were accused of rigging rates, running poor schedules, and causing prices of nearly everything to rise. When it came to paying taxes, they were among the most skilled tax-dodgers.

One year, for example, the railroad paid taxes on only $22 million at a time when it reported capital of $143 million.[19]

A comment uttered by Vanderbilt in October 1882 didn't improve his dismal public image. His attempt to explain what he meant by "the public be damned" made matters even worse: "What does the public care for the railroads except to get as much out of 'em for as small a consideration as possible?... Of course, we like to do everything possible for the benefit of humanity in general, but when we do, we first see that we are benefiting ourselves ..." His words made great copy for headlines across the country and triggered a new battle cry against the excesses of big business and monopolies like the New York Central.[20]

Sensational news accounts of Central train wrecks, collisions, and derailments didn't help either. The railroad's reputation was so bad that Vanderbilt regularly received death threats, some actually describing the exact time and place where he would be shot or stabbed.[21] Finally, in May 1883 Vanderbilt decided to remove himself from the public eye. He resigned from the railroad's presidency and appointed his sons Cornelius II and William K. to key operating positions.[22] The elder Vanderbilt didn't give up his place as a company director.

Six years after his father's death, William claimed to be the richest man in the world. "I am worth one hundred ninety-four million dollars," he bragged to a friend.[23] Indeed, he had nearly doubled his father's fortune. His annual tax-free income from dividends on railroad stocks and interest on government bonds amounted to $10,350,000, an incredible $28,000 a day. It was no stretch for him to offer to cancel a $150,000 loan he made to Ulysses S. Grant, the former U.S. president who was near bankruptcy (Grant declined the offer).[24]

In 1884, a fierce rate war broke out between the New York Central and its archrival, the Pennsylvania Railroad. The conflict threatened to bankrupt both railroads in the midst of a severe economic depression. In July, 1885 J.P. Morgan, by then a director of the Central, arranged a peace conference between the two warring factions aboard his yacht, the *Corsair*, a vessel about the size of a small battleship. The yacht's passengers included Chauncey Depew, the railroad's lawyer, and two top executives of the Pennsylvania Railroad.[25]

As the *Corsair* cruised up and down the East River and New York Harbor, an agreement was struck whereby the "Pennsy," as it was known, would sell its stock in the West Shore Line, a railroad designed to compete with the Central, to a group that included J.P. Morgan and Depew. In return, the Central agreed to halt construction on its planned South Pennsylvania Railroad. The Central would be repaid for the money it had invested in its effort to undermine the Pennsy. Both railroads agreed not to compete except on the New York–Chicago route. The deal simply ignored a Pennsylvania state law that prohibited any railroad from purchasing a parallel or competing line.

Within a few months of the *Corsair* deal, William H. Vanderbilt was dead, a victim of heart failure. His will split control of the family's fortune between his two oldest sons, Cornelius II and William K. Vanderbilt.[26] The two brothers inherited enough stock in the Central to ensure continued family control. Their father had extended the railroad, mostly by shrewd acquisitions, to cover the wealthiest portion of the United States. From New York City, the Central ran on both sides of the Hudson River to Albany, the state's capital. From there, the line ran along the Mohawk River until it reached Buffalo and then west to Chicago. Other Vanderbilt lines extended from Chicago and St. Louis while still others ran from Detroit through Michigan and Indiana.

In the process of building this railroad empire both Vanderbilts, the Commodore and his son William, were admired—and feared—more than any public official. Some looked at them as great entrepreneurs who created new businesses but others saw them as ruthless "robber barons," or "railrogues"[27] who accumulated immense wealth on the backs of workers who faced unsafe working conditions and unfair labor practices.

Although Friedrich Horstmann was a loyal Central employee, he probably harbored mixed feelings about the controversial Vanderbilts. On the one hand, he could tell Henry that they were simply evidence that America was a place of unlimited opportunity. But on the other hand, the capitalist tycoons had accumulated unimaginable amounts of wealth that was difficult to justify, especially in light of their association with various scandals and corruption.

What about working conditions on the Central? The company's view was that an employee accepted the risks of his trade when he took a job on the railroad. Workers were responsible for their own safety—the railroad was not liable for their well-being. It was a view also shared by the legal system of the time. If a worker was killed, a generous railroad owner might provide a few dollars to the widow but that was the extent of it.[28]

Cartoon character resembling William H. Vanderbilt portrays railroad's attitude toward their employees' safety (Harper's Weekly)

PRESIDENT (*to anxious Applicant for a situation as Brakeman*). "Want a berth, eh!—(*to Book-keeper*)—Mr. JONES, has there been a Brakeman killed on the road within a day or two?"
Mr. JONES. "Well, no, Sir, none this week."
PRESIDENT (*to Applicant*). "Ah! well, my man, call next Monday, and by that time I guess there'll be a vacancy."

From the railroad owners' perspective, their workers were merely the "raw material" of their businesses. Commodore Vanderbilt once derided George Westinghouse, Jr.'s compressed air brake system, saying he had no time to waste on "damn fools" who thought a train could be stopped by the wind.[29] And William H. Vanderbilt rejected a petition signed by 450 of his engineers to stop running trains on Sundays because the seven-day work week was ruining their health.[30]

Enginemen like Friedrich Horstmann understood that they shouldered the inherent risks of their jobs. It was an inherent trade-off for the benefits of good pay and prestige—locomotive engineers were the highest paid railroad workers and enjoyed a high status both inside and outside of railroad circles.[31] In a sense, they were "labor aristocrats." Friedrich's loyalty extended both to his employer and to his union, a view that he likely passed on to his aspiring nephew while encouraging him to always support his union, the Brotherhood of Locomotive Engineers (BLE).

Many engineers believed their interests were identical to those of the railroads they served. That was certainly the view of their union, the BLE, whose president P.M. Arthur argued there was no such thing as antagonism between capital and labor: "The working man of today may be the capitalist five or ten years from now," he opined.[32] In fact, the BLE had a history of good relations with the Central going back to 1875, when the two organizations signed the first recorded pay agreement in the railroad industry.[33]

In 1885 Chauncey Depew, the railroad's longtime lawyer and lobbyist, was named president of the New York Central. J.P. Morgan, a director of the company, controlled the railroad's finances. The railroad regained its financial health and began hiring again. Labor strife and the rapid expansion of rail lines had produced thousands of railroad men known as "boomers," men who drifted around the country, working first for one railroad and then another.[34] But the Central's managers wanted reliable, physically fit men under the age of twenty-five who could keep the trains rolling. Firemen were crucial to running their trains; making steam required strength and a skilled and practiced hand. A seasoned fireman with a solid record was a good candidate for eventual promotion to an engineer's position. The Central had no difficulty hiring whoever it wanted; few regulations existed regarding railroad jobs—the railroad could hire firemen simply by concluding that an applicant was honest, sober, and of good moral character.

Many young men, especially farm boys like Henry, responded to "the call of the locomotive," foregoing jobs in other professions.[35] Despite its obvious hazards, well-publicized accounts of bravery by engineers conferred a certain aura of excitement to the work. One such instance occurred in April 1887 when Central engineer Edward Kennar's night freight ran into a landslide near St. Johnsville, New York. Before the engineer died in the wreckage, he managed to wave off a passenger train coming from the opposite direction to prevent another tragedy. The throttle from his engine was proudly displayed in the BLE's Albany Lodge.[36]

Word that the Central was finally hiring reached Henry, probably from his uncle. Ever hopeful, Henry left the McMichael farm and moved to Schenectady, where his younger brother Fred, who had arrived from Hille in 1883, worked as an apprentice. The brothers rented a room together at the Union House, a Spartan boarding place in the city where working men, many of them immigrants, lived two to a room and shared some basic washing and dining facilities.

Henry faced a hiring process that could be influenced in many ways—by political connections, recommendations from prominent men, and even outright bribery of company officials. But it was also driven by direct family connections. In fact, most railroads preferred to hire relatives of employees. Family-based workers, the railroads felt, were likely to be more diligent and loyal to the company.[37]

As a loyal, respected engineer on the Central, Friedrich Horstmann was an ideal sponsor for Henry. But even without his uncle's backing, Henry was exactly the type of man the railroad sought—a healthy, sober individual who thrived on outdoor work and was coolheaded and steady. The fire in his belly to become an engineer was obvious.

Sometime in late 1887 or early '88, Henry was hired by the New

York Central as a fireman. His railroad career was finally launched and it would begin with one of the toughest jobs in America. Now the twenty-four-year-old immigrant could pursue his dream on "America's Greatest Railroad," a title bestowed on the Central by its own publicist.[38]

Six

FIREBOY ON THE NEW YORK CENTRAL

The fireman generally has longer hours than the engineer, as he has to clean a portion of the polished brass-and-iron work of the engine. He has to throw into the firebox several tons of coal a day, and gets so black that his best friends would not know him when washed up. Those who begin young and are intelligent, and conserve their strength, are at length promoted to be engineers.

"The Every-Day Life of Railroad Men," *The American Railway*, 1888

A monster snowstorm dumped nearly four feet of snow on Schenectady as it relentlessly pummeled the northeastern United States over a four-day period in March 1888. High winds whipped the snow into ten- to fifteen-foot drifts, forcing city dwellers to dig tunnels to reach their homes. The great "Blizzard of '88" created havoc with the New York Central.[1] The railroad's four-track main line was shut down and scores of heroic acts were performed by engineers, firemen, and conductors who rescued passengers from stranded trains.

For a novice railroader like Henry, the blizzard was a rude introduction to the everyday life of a railroad man. Good weather or bad, the demands on a fireman were brutal. Rookie firemen got no sympathy from veteran trainmen who tagged them with names like "fireboy," "ashcat," or "bakehead."

A fireboy's first trip on a moving locomotive was a grueling ordeal that called for all the resources he could muster.[2] Riding the rails for ten or twelve hours in a standing position on a shaking, swaying engine for the first time was a jolting experience. He had to shovel six to eight tons of coal into a moving target, a small door in the firebox, all the while keeping on his feet, his hands blistered by the shovel and his eyes blinded by the red-hot fire. And he had still other duties—shaking the grates, cleaning the ash pan, fixing the fire when bad coal was used, filling oil cans, polishing brass, trimming lamps, and taking on water from track pans. (The latter task, called "jerking water," produced the term "jerkwater town.")[3]

Every Central employee was issued a manual called *"Rules of the Operating Department,"* which opened with a not-so-subtle warning: "to enter or remain in the railroad's service is an assurance of willingness to obey the rules." More than one hundred pages spelled out a dizzying array of rules covering everything from drinking on (or off) the job to the intricate hand, flag, and lamp signals that trainmen had to memorize.[4]

Henry was assigned to the railroad's Mohawk Division, which serviced a one-hundred-mile portion of the Central's so-called "water level route" that penetrated the Appalachian mountains in upstate New York through the only natural breach in a mountain range that extends from Maine to Georgia. Squeezing through a two-thousand-foot cut in the mountains near Fonda, New York, the water level route was the principal route for east–west rail service in the northeastern United States.

New hires were usually assigned to freight trains. Most railroad freight service was irregular, meaning that trains were not scheduled but sent out after they accumulated enough freight. Crews were called on a "first-in, first-out" basis, and the train dispatched under a special order.[5] Freight runs were often behind schedule, causing crews to work as long as forty-eight hours at a stretch. Ten- to twelve-hour workdays were the norm, about the time it took for a freight train to cover 100 to 150 miles.[6] Trains were subject to frequent breakdowns, delays, and accidents—all of which produced frustration, tension, and exhausted crews at the end of a day's work. The hours were long, unpredictable, and unrestricted—there was no limit on the number of hours a trainmen could be required to work.

Work on the most dangerous part of the train was physically exhausting. It taxed one's back, legs, and arms—especially when the train was climbing up a steep incline. One of a fireman's least favorite chores was crawling underneath the locomotive to empty the ash pan—a hazardous undertaking, as evidenced by this accident report:[7]

> The fireman crawled under the engine to hoe out the ash pan; the head brakeman came along, pulled the pin behind the engine and called the engineman to go ahead; the engineer, forgetting that his fireman was under the engine, made an attempt to pull out; then the fireman made an attempt to crawl from under but got no further than his two hands on the rail, and although the engine moved only about five feet it was enough to cut his hands off ...

A typical freight crew consisted of an engineer, fireman, conductor, and brakeman. A crew on a forty-car freight train could number as many as eleven men (the Central sometimes ran as many as fifty cars per freight train). Even though the engineer was paid the highest rate, the conductor was the captain of the train. Stationed in the caboose, he was responsible for the train and its contents.

The fireman was usually assigned to a locomotive by a dispatcher or foreman in the engine-house. On board the train, he came under the authority of the engineer. The fireman managed the output of the steam boiler by responding to the engineman's demands for changes in power as the train picked up speed, climbed hills, changed tracks, and stopped at stations. A skilled fireman could anticipate these changes as he shoveled coal into the firebox and watched the boiler. At the same time, he had to know the signals, curves, and grade crossings just as well as the engineer.

An engineer and his fireman had a sort of master-apprentice

relationship and often formed close personal relationships despite their differences in age and skills.[8] Most enginemen would make an effort to teach their firemen the basics of engine driving. But a few took delight in tormenting newly hired fireboys (one method was to call for more and more coal, forcing the rookie fireman to shovel harder and faster).

Brakemen had the most dangerous job. Riding and coupling cars were the two leading dangers to trainmen, especially on freight trains.[9] Brakemen stood between cars to connect the massive, heavy steel jaws that attached the cars together—all the time praying that the cars wouldn't bang together when the locomotive started or stopped. Their injuries included the loss of fingers or limbs (a brakeman's experience could be determined by the number of fingers he had, or didn't have). Some were crushed to death as they coupled cars. Brakemen rode on the tops of slippery cars where they manually applied the brakes; sometimes they would get knocked off their train as it passed under a low bridge or tunnel.

Henry's pay as a fireman was based on the number of miles he traveled on a given day. If he traveled one hundred miles, he would be paid about two cents per mile; if less than one hundred miles, he was guaranteed the amount for a hundred miles. So as long as he was on a moving train he could earn more than two dollars a day. In 1892, firemen earned an average of $2.13 a day, enginemen $3.85.[10]

Unfortunately, trainmen were paid only for the time they put in on a running train. Layovers and work on the engine before and after its run didn't count for pay purposes. The railroad didn't have to pay overtime, thereby saving the cost of extra wages and sometimes getting, in effect, double duty out of its train crews. And layovers were frequent—once crew members reached their destination, they were required to wait for a return train to take them home. Depending on how busy things were, a crew could be stranded for three or four days without pay. If times were busy, a trainman could be ordered to turn around and take a train back to his home base—with no opportunity to rest or eat—and then to join another train on its way out.

Layovers meant that trainmen spent much of their free time away from home, a fact that rendered them susceptible to the booze and women that tempted lonely men in every railroad town. The Central's "Rule G" was well-known: "The use of intoxicants, or the frequenting of places where they are sold, is sufficient cause for dismissal." To entice men away from the saloons and flop houses, YMCAs sprouted up in towns and cities along the railroad's system. They offered cheap, clean rooms with reading areas that provided newspapers and bibles.

Train depots, rail yards, and roundhouses were unsightly places. Some attracted stray dogs, dubbed "raildogs" by workers. One of these canines was a wire-haired terrier named "Railroad Jack" who belonged to a stationmaster at Albany. An adventurous sort, the feisty mutt rode trains from Albany to stations as far away as Buffalo and New York City. When Railroad Jack died, his railroad friends had the famous canine stuffed and put on display.[11]

Like enginemen, firemen were promoted within their trade. They could move up from extra to regular runs, from branch line to main line, and from freight to passenger service. Prospects for advancing up the chain were directly affected by the business cycle, especially the volume of freight traffic, which determined the number of men needed by the railroad. Favoritism and seniority also played a part in winning promotions.

Firemen could be called to work at any time, whether in the middle of the night or on any day of the week, including Sundays. Any time Henry was off duty, he could expect to find a "call boy" at his door ordering him to report to the Yard for work. It was a job not well suited for a married man raising a family.

Trainmen had no paid holidays and vacations. Most railroads viewed retirement and health insurance as impractical socialist ideas. Firemen could buy insurance from the Brotherhood of Locomotive Firemen (BLF), but many were required to buy it from their employers. Some railroads, probably including the New York Central, had compulsory relief plans that required employees to waive their rights to sue the company for damages if they accepted a payout. Workers saw these plans as nothing more than schemes by the railroads to forestall liability suits by those injured on the job, or by families of workers who were killed. Critics dubbed them "self-protection funds" that allowed railroads to raid the dead man's pension fund and hand the widow "her own money, while the world applauds the generosity and fatherly care of the corporation."[12]

Just how dangerous was it to work on a railroad? In 1890, two years after Henry became a fireman, the Interstate Commerce Commission (ICC) published its first nationwide statistics on the causes of casualties sustained by railroad workers. The ICC report revealed that 2,451 workers were killed in 1890 while another 22,396 were injured.[13] The report confirmed that trainmen (engineers, firemen, conductors, and brakemen), who accounted for only about 20 percent of the nation's total railroad work force, held the most dangerous jobs. Their fatality rate, one author writes, "was simply staggering."[14]

But the ICC's reports didn't tell the whole story. They were based on incomplete, voluntary reports from the railroads, some of which didn't even bother to submit any data. Still, the data made it clear that railroad safety was a fast-growing national crisis. It was "a reproach to our civilization," charged President Benjamin Harrison, that railroad workers are subjected to "a peril of life and limb as great as that of a soldier in time of war."[15] In fact, railroad workers in 1890 ran risks that were two and a half times the risk of the most dangerous modern jobs. And it was the men who ran the trains who experienced death rates many times higher than the average railroad employee.[16]

In the early 1890s, the New York Central was overwhelmed with traffic on its system. One report noted that the Central ran 168 trains a day on its main line: Trains "traveling in sight of each other include sixty-car freights without air brakes, locals, and sixty-mile-an-hour expresses," it observed. The *Locomotive News* proposed that the Central, which called itself "America's Greatest Railroad," ought to add "for Rear Collisions" to its title.[17]

Safety simply didn't rank among the Central's priorities. Speed and publicity topped its agenda. On October 26, 1891, the Central launched what it called the first high-speed, long distance passenger train in the world, the *Empire State Express*. It covered the 440 miles between New York and Buffalo in eight hours and forty minutes, at one point clocking a speed of seventy miles an hour. "That such speed can be made in safety and is a regular thing is a striking illustration of the progress made in the science of railroading," applauded the *New York Tribune*.[18]

That success gave the Central's ace publicist, George H. Daniels, an even grander idea—namely, a one-of-a-kind locomotive capable of setting a world speed record. Designed by the Central's William Buchanan and built at the railroad's West Albany shops, engine No. 999 was an American-type 4-4-0 locomotive. Its huge seven-foot two-inch drivers provided the necessary speed. On a trial run between Batavia and Buffalo on May 10, 1893, engineer Charlie Hogan held the throttle wide open and drove the four-car *Empire State Express* over a thirty-six-mile stretch of straight track to a speed of 112.5 miles an hour.

The Central promptly claimed a new world speed record. While some questioned the veracity of the claim, it was the first vehicle ever to carry anyone at a speed in excess of one hundred miles an hour.[19] According to the *Buffalo Evening News,* Hogan "let the monster Columbian engine out a little and broke all records ever made." The canny Daniels put the famous No. 999 at the head of a train called the *Exposition Flyer* and sent it to Chicago to display at the 1893 World's Columbian Exposition. Engine 999, the most famous locomotive of all time, was later memorialized on a U.S. postage stamp.

But the Central's amazing achievement couldn't conceal the mounting death and injury rates on the nation's railroads. In 1893, one in twenty-eight of all railroad workers was injured during the course of the year while one of every 320 was killed. For trainmen, the odds were even worse—one in every nine was injured while one in every 115 was killed.[20] Annual reports of gruesome figures like these prompted a public outcry for a new national law to require safety improvements on trains.

Leading the charge was a former railroad agent, Lorenzo Coffin, who was also a Christian chaplain. He gave speeches, wrote articles, and even rode freight trains to gather testimony from railroad workers. Dismissed by the railroads as that "little farmer from Iowa," Father Coffin brought a religious fervor to the cause: "It was God behind the movement," he said, after Congress finally passed the Safety Appliance Act in 1893.[21]

The new law required railroads to install automatic couplers on freight cars to eliminate the need for trainmen to go between cars. A reasonable number of cars on a train were to be equipped with air brakes so an engineer could better control his train. Grab irons were to be installed to prevent trainmen from falling off moving trains.

The new regulations brought howls of protest from the railroads, who claimed the safety devices were too costly.[22] A more cynical reason was that they simply didn't want the expense of buying and installing them. Why should they buy automatic car couplers when, as one state railroad commission put it, "it costs nothing to get another brakeman when one is disabled or killed, while patent couplers are expensive." Congress, the railroads charged, had approved an unnecessary and unwarranted intervention in their business. *Railway Age*, an industry publication, denounced the new law—accidents, it pronounced, were simply "the price being paid for civilization." Another publication, *Railroad Gazette*, proclaimed that the issues involved were too "scientific" for the government.

While they protested, the crafty railroads engineered a roundhouse-sized loophole in the new law that prevented its main provisions from going into effect until January 1, 1898. This meant that trainmen like Henry Horstman would not have the full protection of the new federal safety law until the turn of the century. The railroads could simply take their time installing proven safety devices like automatic couplers and the Westinghouse air brake system.

Every trainman knew a fellow worker who was injured or killed on the job. That realization hung like a dark and foreboding cloud over his daily work. It was a tough life, a long day, and as one locomotive manufacturer put it, "a game that calls for all the stuff a man has in him."[23] Still, Henry was determined to reach his ultimate goal—the engineer's seat on the right side of the cab. Hard work was nothing new to the determined immigrant, although he didn't know he would spend nearly a decade shoveling coal into the fireboxes of lurching trains before he finally achieved his American Dream.

Seven

LIFE AND DEATH IN ELECTRIC CITY

Schenectady was never the same after Tom Edison came to town.

Larry Hart, *Schenectady's Golden Era*, 1974

Soon after the great "Blizzard of '88," a bustling new manufacturing plant, the Edison Machine Works, became so busy in Schenectady that its eight hundred hired hands were literally standing on one another's feet. The company was a brainchild of Thomas Alva Edison, who had moved his manufacturing plant out of New York City, away from high rents and the meddling of labor and political bosses, to property he quietly bought up in the city.[1]

Other businesses also prospered in the city. The Mica Insulator Company opened its doors a few blocks away from the Edison Machine Works. The Schenectady Agricultural Works, founded by George Westinghouse, Sr., manufactured farm equipment in a plant along the Erie Canal (Westinghouse's son invented the air brake system once ridiculed by Commodore Vanderbilt). Smaller businesses like C.F. Horstmann & Company, owned by Louisa's uncle Carl, produced brooms and brushes made out of local broomcorn. *"Fancy Striped Broom Handles a Specialty,"* was the company's advertising theme.

Henry's job with the New York Central galvanized him to apply for citizenship in his adopted homeland. In a petition filed on July 30,

1888, he renounced his allegiance to "William II, King of Prussia and Emperor of United Germany" and pledged to support the United States Constitution.[2] The statement was witnessed by his uncle Friedrich, who had been naturalized in 1859, and John Slater, another fireman on the Central. They testified that Henry had lived in America for at least five years and was "a person of good moral character" (U.S. law denied citizenship to specified "undesirables" such as habitual drunkards, polygamists, gamblers, and convicts). The youthful applicant signed his petition Henry Horstmann (he later "Americanized" his surname by spelling it with a single "n").

With Henry's new status as an American citizen came the right to vote, an opportunity that didn't exist in his former homeland where emperors were crowned, not elected. In fact, the local German-speaking community was abuzz with talk about William II, a pompous twenty-eight-year-old hothead who unexpectedly succeeded his father, Crown Prince Friedrich Wilhelm. The latter, a popular ruler, died in 1888 after only a hundred days on the throne.[3]

At the same time, American voters were in the process of choosing a president of the United States. Rumor had it that the Central's own president, Chauncey Depew, had his eyes set on the White House. It's not likely that Depew was a favorite among immigrant citizens like Henry as he was clearly hostile to the foreign-born.[4] On the stump, the railroad chieftain exploited the public's fear of foreigners, sparked largely by an anarchist bombing at Haymarket Square in Chicago two years earlier. "The country cannot afford to become the dumping-ground of the world for its vicious or ignorant or worthless or diseased. Only the better, more enlightened emigrants should be welcomed,"[5] he thundered. Depew conveniently ignored the fact that among the Central's 20,659 employees[6] were many men like Henry Horstman, "worthless" immigrants by his standard, who ran the railroad's trains, built its bridges and tunnels, and laid its track.

Depew's presidential ambition reached its peak at the Republican Party's convention in Chicago, held in June 1888. His bid to become the party's standard bearer was opposed by delegates from crucial western and farming states who wanted nothing to do with a candidate associated with the Vanderbilt system. One delegate observed that Depew had a "damnable record as a jobber and corruptionist" as a lobbyist for the New York Central.[7]

A suggestion that Depew be nominated for vice president because he would have the backing of the Vanderbilts and the New York Central interests went nowhere.[8] If anything, that notion raised alarm bells with many delegates. As one delegate noted, the sight of Depew surrounded by railroad men was "a frightening reminder of where his interests lay."[9] In the end, when it became clear that Depew couldn't muster enough votes, the Central's president withdrew his name from the balloting. The Republicans nominated Benjamin Harrison, who went on to defeat Grover Cleveland in the 1888 presidential election.

As Schenectady prospered, optimism soared among its residents. The city was growing faster than anyone could have imagined. By 1890, its population had soared to 19,902, a gain of more than 6,200 residents in a decade.[10] The strong economy kicked off a marriage boom among the Horstmann immigrants. Within a year or two, Henry's brother (Fred) married Rose Gerding, and Louisa's brother (Charles) wed Clara Panthen. Louisa's sister (Marie) married Henry Lange, a cabinetmaker from Hille.

This outburst of Horstmann nuptials was apparently not lost on Henry and Louisa. The couple planned to be married once Henry landed a job on the railroad. The longtime sweethearts were adventurous, ambitious, and fully committed to each other. They had no reason to wait any longer. Henry's job appeared stable and Louisa could work in her uncle's tailor shop.

The merging of two separate and distinct Horstmann families with roots deep in the "Old Country" was an occasion to celebrate. A German tradition called for relatives and friends to surprise an engaged couple with a *Polterabend*, or "an evening of broken porcelain." A noisy scene would ensue as the hosts smashed old kitchenware in front of the future bride and groom. The event evoked the German proverb *Scherben bringen Gluck* ("broken pieces bring you luck"). Still another wedding custom, or *Hochzeit brauche*, required a couple to demonstrate how they could work together and manage difficult situations.

Henry and Louisa were married in the German Methodist Church at the corner of Union and Lafayette streets. Pastor J.C. Deininger performed the ceremony on April 30, 1890.[11] The church was crowded with Horstmann relatives, their families, and well-wishers from a German-American community that included many Hille immigrants. It's likely that Henry's brother was his best man while Mary Lange, Louisa's sister, served as her maid of honor.

The newlyweds rented an apartment at 745 State Street, a location not far from the city's train depot. Within a few months, Henry found a house for sale on Mynderse Street in the city's Fourth Ward. It was a two-story frame structure with two bedrooms on each floor. The interior boasted a coal-fired stove in the kitchen and a coal-burning furnace in the basement. Its backyard had ample space for a garden. Best of all, the upstairs could be rented out.

Henry struck a deal with the owner of the house, Albert Bigwood, a machinist at the city's Electric Works. He managed to scrape together all but $368 to buy the house, a sum which he agreed to pay within one year at 6 percent interest.[12] It was a big step for the newlyweds given that Henry earned only about sixty dollars a month.

But the newlywed's joy at owning their own house was short lived. On August 9, 1890, one day after Henry signed his mortgage papers, a strike was called against the New York Central by the Knights of Labor (KOL)—a union that represented most of the railroad's shopmen, freight handlers, and switchmen.[13] It was a rude awakening for Henry and included his first exposure to words like "fink" and "scab."

The dispute was triggered when the Central fired twenty experienced men who the company claimed were performing unsatisfactory work. The strike began in New York City and quickly spread to stations along the Hudson River and Harlem lines of the Central. Work stoppages quickly reached Albany and shut down the West Albany Yard, the Central's vital nerve center.

Louisa Horstmann (on right) with her sister, Mary Lange. Standing is Clara Panthen, Louisa's sister-in-law. Photo ca. 1890.

In an attempt to control the situation in Albany, the railroad hired two hundred Pinkertons (private armed mercenaries) to protect strikebreakers, or "scabs," from the strikers. The Pinkertons rode into Albany's Union Station on the tops of freight cars, brandishing Winchester rifles. Apparently without provocation, the hired guns fired into a peaceful crowd of strikers picketing the station, killing a woman and injuring a disabled person. In the ensuing chaos, the trigger-happy Pinkertons (called "finks" by the strikers) charged into the demonstrators, killing five people.[14]

A public outcry arose against the Pinkertons' strong-arm tactics.

Albany police arrested many, charging them with assault, attempted murder, and disorderly conduct. An Albany newspaper accused the Central of importing "bruisers and thugs ... from the slums of New York."[15] The state legislature called for an investigation into the incident and other abuses attributed to the already unpopular railroad.

Seeking to expand the strike, the KOL sought support from the Brotherhood of Locomotive Firemen (BLF), a union Henry had likely joined. The Central's negotiator told newspapers the company would replace firemen and any others who struck, adding that the New York Central would go out of business rather than give in to the strikers. But the firemen had little interest in striking. They were satisfied with their wages; some of them earned $85 a month and didn't find that a reason to strike.[16] Likewise, Uncle Friedrich's engineers wanted nothing to do with the Knights, who had ordered the strike without support from that powerful brotherhood. The BLE had good working relations with the Central and regarded the Knights as troublemakers. On August 12, a freight train with twenty-eight loaded cars departed from Schenectady, heading west on the Mohawk Division. Its departure was a signal that the strike would not hold.[17]

The New York Central had no intention of giving up its right to hire and fire whomever it wanted. The railroad declared it would do whatever was necessary to squelch the strike, even if it had to spend as much as two million dollars. The company's board of directors included two Vanderbilt brothers, financier J.P. Morgan, and president Chauncey Depew. The railroad sent an uncompromising message to its workers that it would "fight the present strike to the end. Those who do not work tomorrow will be considered as having left service and their places will be filled as soon as possible."[18]

A few weeks later, a New York Central passenger train bound for Montreal was derailed, the result of a rail mysteriously placed crosswise on the track. Miraculously, no one was killed, although many passengers were injured. In a suspiciously short time, Pinkerton detectives brought three men to Albany, where they confessed to the sabotage, saying they did it at the KOL's request. Although they were never convicted, the incident did great harm to the Knights' public image.

The Central's deep pockets and patience were simply too much for the Knights. The KOL capitulated, denouncing Chauncey Depew as a "mere figure-head" president who sat back while others did his dirty work. Depew, though, had the last word. The strike's end, he said, was due to "the loyalty and courage of the BLE," shrewdly crediting the Brotherhood for safeguarding "the public and the corporation against the demands of intemperate violence." The enginemen, he said, were owed a debt of gratitude by the nation for the "courage, fidelity, and intelligence" they displayed in standing by their posts.[19]

The strike over, Henry and Louisa settled into their newly acquired house on Mynderse Street. It was a pleasant working-class neighborhood that included men who were patternmakers, draftsmen, machinists, and carpenters. Spouses held jobs that ranged from hatters to stenographers. Many residents were first-generation immigrants from Germany, as well as Scotland, England, Ireland, and Switzerland.

The house was within walking distance of a new railroad depot, an odd-shaped brick structure with two mosquelike domes, where Henry could board a train for the West Albany Yard. Or he could take a horse-drawn trolley to the station for a five-cent fare. An electric-powered trolley, operated by a new company, Schenectady Railway, also offered service to main points in the city. Henry and his uncle likely traveled together to the West Albany Yard to get their train assignments. After finishing their runs, they could stop in a local saloon just outside the gate to order beer and talk shop with other trainmen, machinists, and yard workers.

At home in the evening, Louisa prepared *abendessen*, a supper of German-style wieners and bolognas, or homemade sausages on their coal-fired stove. She bought her favorite meats from Dieterich's or Behan's, both nearby meat markets. She beat and mixed their food by hand and did the dishwashing. Food was kept cool in summer with an ice refrigerator, an upright box that contained a foot-square chunk of ice, which lasted about a week.

After supper, Louisa scrubbed Henry's work clothes while he took a bath in a cast-iron, claw-footed tub to remove layers of black soot he acquired from firing engines. She scrubbed clothes in a tub with a washboard using yellow bars of laundry soap—no detergents, or even soap flakes, existed at the time.

Trainmen living who worked for the New York Central were part of a close-knit community. Like combat veterans, they shared experiences that were not comprehensible to those who worked elsewhere. They spent what little free time they had outside of their demanding jobs socializing with each other and with each other's families.

Henry's well-known uncle lived on Liberty Street, close to the railroad depot. There he could meet famous Central engineers like Reuben Allen, who drove the *William H. Vanderbilt* on the maiden run of the Central's *Fast Mail;* and Thomas Dormady, a veteran who was at the throttle of the *Empire State Express* when it made its first run. Henry was surely in awe of these well-known and highly regarded enginemen.

Early in 1891, an epidemic of typhoid fever swept through Schenectady, probably spread by water carrying typhoid germs from the Mohawk River. The city's water supply, pumped from a powerhouse at the foot of Ferry Street, distributed death to every section of the city.[20] No effective treatment or vaccine was available to treat the disease other than putting the sick person under quarantine. The creation of penicillin, sulfa drugs, and antibiotics was half a century away. Doctors of the day believed that death from the disease was the result of poor genetics or "spiritual failure." Most of its unfortunate victims died within a few short weeks.

It was surely a frightening time for Henry and Louisa, who had lived in the city for less than a year. They had plenty of reason to be concerned. Not only was Louisa pregnant with their first child, but word came that Uncle Friedrich had suddenly contracted the dreaded disease.

By the end of January, the epidemic had taken the life of fifty-six-year-old Friedrich Horstmann. An obituary mourned the engineer's death as "an irreparable loss to his family, and to the railroad company he has so long and faithfully served and to this community in which he continued to reside until the last."

Schenectady Daily Union
January 28, 1891

His death removes one of the best railroad men from the service of the New York Central and Hudson River Railroad. For 36 years he has been with that company, dating from the time of the Albany and Utica Division. His specialty for many years has been the running of express trains between Albany and Syracuse. In this relation, he was unsurpassed for a strict and conscientious fidelity to duty. He was numbered among the senior passenger engineers of this city, and had the late Reuben Allen for an associate, together with Thomas Dormady, Jacob Vrooman and possibly a few others. Mr. Horstmann was so devoted to his arduous, responsible trust as to have neither time nor inclination for civic work. He was known as an excellent citizen but never held public office for which he was well qualified. In connection with his life's work, he became a member of the Brotherhood of Locomotive Engineers ...

Friedrich Horstmann's wife, Caroline, was left with six girls under the age of eighteen. They had three other children, including twenty-year-old Jessie, a school teacher.

The sudden loss of his uncle was certainly a shock to Henry. The seemingly indestructible man who drove the Central's most advanced locomotives was the sole inspiration for his American Dream. A surrogate father as well as a mentor, Friedrich had taken him under his wing a decade earlier and was at his side when he became a United States citizen.

No doubt Henry and Louisa took solace in the German Methodist

Church where they were married. A few months later, the young couple's first child was born. They named her Jessie after Friedrich's daughter.

In 1891, a group of German-Americans met in Wincke's Tavern and established a Schenectady *Turn Verein* to preserve German customs, language and celebrations.[21] Ostensibly a gymnastic club (its motto was "Sound Body—Sound Mind"), Turner Hall on Center Street became the social center of the German community, a place where new arrivals could learn about life in America. The Turners strongly defended their language: "Honor the German language," they urged. "The spirit of your forefathers is preserved in its words!" It was a refrain that appeared in Turner halls across the United States.[22]

In 1892, the Edison Machine Works merged with other electrical businesses to create the General Electric Company. In just six years, the city once known as "Old Dorp" was transformed into a modern "Electric City." Word about job opportunities in Schenectady brought a surge of new immigrants, most from Southern and Eastern Europe, to the city, boosting its foreign population and challenging an undermanned police force. Schenectady newspapers had a field day with the new arrivals, reporting their difficulties as Italians and Poles began to show up in police arrest books. Headlines like *"Me Kill-A-You"* and *"Me Take-a-You Life,"* along with stories about brawls at Polish weddings, created an impression that the newcomers were more inclined to crime than the earlier immigrants, even though they were no more disorderly than others.[23]

Ethnic communities sprouted throughout the city. The new arrivals wanted to live near people who spoke their language and shared their customs. German-American bakers, butchers, cigar makers, and cabinetmakers first settled in the city's First Ward. Still other German-speaking immigrants settled in the townships of Mount Pleasant, Rotterdam, Scotia, and Niskayuna.

By 1890, 22 percent of the city's 19,902 residents were foreign-born. Some 2,531 of these were born in Germany, the largest of any other immigrant group.[24] That count didn't include German-speaking immigrants who came from countries like Austria and Switzerland, all part of a German cultural area called the "Deutschtum." However measured, the German influence in Schenectady was unmistakable. Strolling German bands, which usually played in the springtime, performed songs like this classic:[25]

> *Dot Leedle German band, dot leedle German band;*
> *De beoble cry and say, "Oh my!" as ve march drough de land.*
> *Ve go around de streeds almost every day,*
> *Und set de beoble vild mit de music dot ve blay;*
> *"Good-by Sourheart," und "Hime Sweed Hime," ve blay so fine,*
> *But ve always do our best ven ve blay "Die Wacht am Rhein."*

Another popular ditty—sung wherever beer was consumed—incorporated German music but was rendered in English:

> *Oh vhere, oh vhere iss mein little dog gone,*
> *Oh vhere, oh vhere can he be?*
> *'Mit his ears cut shord und his tail cut long—*
> *Oh vhere, oh vhere can he be?*

As popular as these songs were, German-Americans still felt threatened by "Amerikanizers" who objected to schools and churches that taught and prayed in foreign languages. Although most German-born residents had learned English, they had no desire to give up their native language. They enjoyed reading German language newspapers, the *Schenectady Deutscher Anzeiger,* published from 1876 to 1896, and a successor, the weekly *Das Deutsche Journal.*[26]

Early Anglo-Dutch settlers in the city wanted to impose their values on the foreign-born population. They criticized Germans for working on Sundays in violation of the Sabbath, even though many railroad workers like Henry had no choice in the matter. The English looked at beer-drinking Germans as major obstacles to a prohibition agenda aimed at shutting down saloons and the sale of all alcoholic beverages. Not surprisingly, Germans (and Irish, too) didn't take kindly to this superior attitude—they hadn't left their European homelands to be told by puritan preachers what they could do in their free time.[27]

As the year 1893 arrived, the ethnic differences in Electric City took a back seat to a looming economic crisis that threatened the livelihoods of many city residents. The deep, nationwide depression would last four years and nearly wipe out Henry's American Dream.

Eight

AN EXTRAVAGANT DEPRESSION

*The spectacle of men fighting for work ... My God! This
is terrible! Battling for the privilege of working all day for
enough to eat—and the next day to go at it again; and
so on until the earth rattles on their pine boxes.*

Ignatius Donnelly in *The Representative*, August 29, 1894

A few months after Henry's twenty-ninth birthday in October 1892,
a financial panic gripped the nation. Consumers quit buying,
retailers cancelled orders, factories shut down, and workers in virtually
every industry lost their jobs. In the first six months of 1893, 360 banks
and eight thousand businesses failed while the stock market collapsed.
Crowds stood at brokerage houses to watch their investments shrink.
Foreclosures and bank failures triggered a run on banks as the credit
system seized up, a situation eerily similar to the current 2008-'09
crisis.[1]

The nation lurched into a depression that destroyed many railroads
and undermined the business of those like the New York Central,
forcing them to slash their workforce. By 1894, 192 railroads with about
forty-one thousand miles of track—almost one fourth of the entire U.S.
rail system—were in various stages of bankruptcy.[2] Among these were
the Philadelphia and Reading, Union-Pacific, Northern-Pacific, and
Santa Fe railroads. J.P. Morgan and his fellow financiers reorganized

failed lines, bringing them under banker control, or "Morganizing" almost every bankrupt railroad east of the Mississippi.[3]

Labor conflicts erupted across the nation, including a strike against railroads in 1894, triggered when George Pullman slashed wages and hiked rents in his company town outside of Chicago.[4] Led by a fiery labor leader named Eugene Debs, The American Railway Union (ARU) shut down rail arteries from Chicago to the West Coast. Rail traffic in the west ground to a halt as 260,000 workers walked out. Battles with state and federal troops broke out. Pullman refused to compromise and the ARU, unable to present a united front against the company, collapsed. The strike was broken, and its leaders (including Debs) were imprisoned while other strikers were blacklisted. Although the strike didn't directly impact the Central, its message was clear—railroad workers who went out on strike would be punished.

The brutal depression produced unemployment rates of 25 percent or more in some urban areas, putting it on a par with the Great Depression that would come later, in the 1930s. Throughout the country, stories of despair and suicide flooded the newspapers. Families broke up as men took to the rails and the roads to search for work. The unemployed and homeless became wanderers, called tramps or "hobos" (a corruption of "Hello, Boy!"), who hitched rides on freight trains. The trains were rolling symbols of the desperation faced by an estimated three million men out of work across the nation. The tramps slipped into rail cars and jumped off at the outskirts of a town or city, later appearing at the back doors of houses to beg for food or work. Some never made it that far and fell to their death. Railroads set up police forces to eject hitchhikers from their trains.

Even the United States government was in danger of bankruptcy. The public's demand to exchange paper money for gold triggered a huge drain on the Treasury Department's reserves. As gold reserves plunged, President Grover Cleveland desperately searched for a way to stanch the bleeding. He turned to the one man in the country who could command the resources necessary to prevent bankruptcy: J. P. Morgan—the financier, deal maker, and director of countless companies, among them the New York Central and Hudson River Railroad.

Morgan proposed that the United States Treasury buy gold coins from his firm and pay for them with newly issued government bonds.[5] Sure enough, gold began to flow back into the Treasury as investors showed they had more confidence in Morgan than they did in the U.S. government. Soon after, however, charges arose that Morgan reaped an apparently legal but exorbitant multimillion-dollar profit from the deal. The American people, charged William Jennings Bryan, owed President Cleveland the sort of gratitude that "a passenger feels toward a trainman who had opened a switch and precipitated a wreck."[6]

The economic disaster became known as the "Cleveland Depression" and it generated widespread public outrage over the wealth and power concentrated in the hands of people like the Vanderbilts, J.P. Morgan, John Rockefeller, and Andrew Carnegie. Influential magazines like *McClure's* and *Cosmopolitan* became the advance guard of a new Progressive movement that called for busting up the trusts in railroads, steel, and oil.

Journalists exposed the extravagant lifestyles led by the robber barons. These revealing accounts outraged the public at a time when four-fifths of the nation's families earned less than $500 a year.[7] The Vanderbilts, heirs to the fortunes built by their father and grandfather, were prime targets. Within ten years of William H. Vanderbilt's death, his four sons erected mansions and country estates beyond anything ever seen in the United States.[8]

Cornelius II, the oldest of William's sons, tore down townhouses over an entire block of Fifth Avenue in New York, replacing them with the biggest mansion on the Avenue. The press scolded him, saying, "he has no business in a Republic to flaunt his wealth so insolently." Undeterred, he built a summer cottage in Newport, Rhode Island, spending $7 million to hire two thousand laborers, artisans, and artists. Modeled after a North Italian villa, "The Breakers" featured a morning room built in France, disassembled there, and sent to Newport complete with a crew of French installers.

William K. "Willie" Vanderbilt and his wife, Alva, commissioned a chateau at Fifty-second Street. Built in the gaudy style of the great mansions of fifteenth-century France, it became the standard for mansions on Fifth Avenue and the palatial homes of Newport. Willie also built an immense oceangoing yacht, the largest private ship afloat, complete with steel cabins, mahogany paneling, a library, and a dining saloon.

Not to be outdone, Frederick W. Vanderbilt, who lived in a Fifth Avenue mansion given to him by his father, built yet another in Newport. "Rough Point" was a place where he could sail his English-built yacht, the *Conqueror*. His summer retreat was a fifty-room Italian Renaissance mansion on six hundred acres in Hyde Park, New York that overlooked the Hudson River.

George Vanderbilt, the youngest of the four, bought five thousand acres of land near Ashville, in the Great Smoky Mountains of North Carolina, to get away from the cold New York City winters. He later expanded his acquisition to a grand total of 228 square miles and constructed a country estate in the style of a great French chateau that covered five acres, about the size of the Grand Central Depot. Stocked with priceless treasures from his European jaunts, the 250-room "Biltmore" was (and still is) the largest private home ever built in America.

Despite the depression, the Vanderbilts' railroads and other investments "earned money faster than any human being could spend it."[9] And there was no income tax to trim their tidal wave of wealth. Their widely publicized opulence and wealth was surely incomprehensible to men like Henry who worked for the giant railroad. Even the best-paid Central engineers earned a mere $2,000 a year, an amount that wouldn't buy a week's feed for Willie Vanderbilt's horses, a man who once complained that wealth was a real handicap to happiness.

Like most industrial cities, Schenectady struggled through the turbulent economic times. Locomotive production plunged as the Big Shop lost orders from bankrupt railroads. A local German newspaper, *Deutsche Anzeiger*, shut down its presses and went out of business. The newly formed General Electric Company survived, mostly because of its ability to produce new products created by ingenious inventors like Charles Steinmetz, a German immigrant who fled his homeland to avoid political persecution for his socialist writings.[10]

A brilliant mathematician, Steinmetz was nearly deported when he disembarked at Castle Garden because of his misshapen appearance (he was less than five feet tall and handicapped by a twisted torso). He arrived in Schenectady in mid-1893 and became known as the "Electric Wizard" for his work on electric current.

Despite the difficult times, life in the city weathered the economic storm.[11] The Schenectady Railway Company extended its streetcar routes; new electric streetlights were installed to brighten downtown at night; and a new elementary school, the Union Street School, opened its doors. Adventurous boys played "bendies" in the spring, running across the semi-frozen Erie Canal to get to the other side before the sagging ice gave way. Charles Steinmetz worked at his summer camp on the Mohawk River, where he entertained guests, one of whom was Mabel Horstmann, a daughter of Friedrich Horstmann, Henry's uncle.

Louie Nicholaus and his wife Sophie, an energetic pair of German immigrants, opened a classic German-style café in 1895. Nicholaus came to Schenectady from Baden, Germany. He first worked in the Big Shop only to be injured later in a railroad accident. Their saloon and "eating bar," Nicholaus's German Restaurant, became the most popular gathering place in town, famous for its free lunches, German strudel, and nickel-a-glass beer.

The Nicholaus saloon survived despite prohibitionists' attempts to dry out cities and towns with large populations of beer-loving Germans and Irish. The English felt they alone had the right to decide the correct "American" way of life and had some success in passing laws to shut down saloons and force certain sections of the city (as well as neighboring townships like Scotia) to go totally dry. German-Americans took those actions as an attack on their freedom and traditions.[12]

The Horstmann families weathered the depression as best they could. Charles Horstmann managed a drug store on Wall Street while his sisters Jessie, Grace, and Mabel taught school and lived with their widowed mother on Liberty Street. Louisa's uncle Christian maintained his tailor shop while her other uncle, C.F. Horstmann, branched out from broom-making to manufacturing silk, mittens, and gloves. Henry's brother Fred held on to his job as a machinist

But times were especially difficult for railroad men like Henry. His employer was financially fit enough to survive the economic turmoil, but freight traffic, the backbone of the railroad's far-flung system, fell to record low levels. When the Central ran fewer trains, it needed fewer trainmen. Only the most senior enginemen and firemen could count on steady work. With less than ten years seniority, Henry was poorly positioned for steady work. Fewer runs and long stretches of time without work translated into sharply reduced take-home pay. The average annual pay of a fireman on the Central in the first year of the depression amounted to just $642,[13] an amount that certainly declined as freight traffic plummeted in subsequent years. To make ends meet, Henry likely returned to the McMichael's farm for work as his prospects for promotion to engineer, or even keeping his fireman's job, appeared to slip away.

The depression years were hard on Henry's family. Louisa's youngest brother (also named Henry) arrived from Hille in 1892 and may have stayed with them for a time. Louisa gave birth to their second child, Clarence, in June 1894. City records show the family moved to another house on Mynderse Street, probably as renters, until they were able to move back into their house a few years later. The times were bad enough that Henry may have wondered whether leaving his former homeland was a wise decision after all.

But the "Old Country" itself offered nothing but sad news. Henry's mother died in February 1894, and in January 1897, his father was buried beside her in the Hille *friedhof*.[14] With the elder Horstmann's passing, the farm at Hille #29 was inherited by Henry's brother, Christian, who with his wife Marie (nee Schütte), had begun to raise a new generation of Horstmanns. They would produce two sons, Christian and Heinrich, before the twentieth century arrived.

Henry's ties to his family in the Old Country faded after his parents' death. He hung a photograph of his father in the living room of his house, perhaps as a reminder of the godsend he received from him when he left Hille #29 in 1881. Like most German-Americans, Henry was devoted to his family and surely regretted that his parents never met his children. Louisa gave birth to their third child, Irene, just a few weeks after his father died.

Did his parents know what their son had accomplished in America? At the very least they surely knew he had married a Hille *Fraulein* and had found a job on the railroad. This information could have come by letter from Henry himself or from neighbors in Hille who also had family members in Schenectady. Even so, his parents died without knowing whether or not their adventurous son had achieved his boyhood dream to become a *lokomotivfuhrer*.

Nine

AT THE THROTTLE

*Perhaps no other occupation ever fetched the American fancy
as did that of the locomotive engineer ... The aviator of a later
generation, a mere mechanic cleaving his wild blue yonder,
was never in the same league with the brave engineer.*

Lucius Beebe and Charles Clegg, *Hear the Train Blow,* 1952

In the fall of 1897, a train carrying William McKinley steamed into
Schenectady's railroad station. The nation's newly elected president
was on his way to Washington, D.C., from his home in Ohio.

When the train clamored to a halt, the president-elect stepped out
and addressed a welcoming crowd, which let out a mighty cheer as he
proclaimed that the end of the "Cleveland Depression" was at hand.
It was welcome news for city dwellers like the Horstmans, who prayed
for an end to the economic disaster.

True to McKinley's prediction, the nation's economy began to
recover from the devastating depression. As business accelerated, freight
and passenger traffic on the nation's railroads surged. The pickup
breathed new life into the New York Central, inspiring the railroad to
order new locomotives and hire more trainmen. And as railroads across
the nation hired more workers, the number of killed and wounded rose
dramatically.

The Central's managers scoured their employment rolls searching for reliable, trustworthy men capable of running locomotives in the fast-changing environment. The railroad especially wanted experienced men who knew how to get the best performance out of an engine. A good engineer could save the company a lot of money by keeping the expenses of engine-running down. His daily wages were a pittance compared to what he could save the railroad by operating his engine without wasting fuel and abusing the machinery.

Archie Buchanan was a famous Central engineer who drove the *Empire State Express* between New York City and Albany. Coming from a railroading family, he was well acquainted with the perils of his profession. One of his three brothers was an engineer killed in a terrible accident near Albany. Another was a master mechanic in the shops at West Albany, and a third, William, was the genius who designed the Central's famous Engine No. 999.[1]

In a candid interview published in *McClure's Magazine*,[2] Buchanan issued a warning to firemen who wanted to move up to an engineer's position. If they did so, Buchanan said, any fireman promoted to engineer would find the first years of his life to be very hard "for he has to run at all sorts of hours, day and night, winter and summer, and on the meanest kind of trains. If this does not kill him," the veteran engineman explained, "he finally becomes engineer on an express and has a better time of it." Still, he said, "a good many of the boys prefer to remain firemen all their lives rather than stand such hardships."

The *McClure's* interview went on: "There may be death lurking around a curve, death spreading its arms in a tunnel, and the engineer must see and be responsible for everything. Not only must he note instantly all that is before him, the signals, switches, bridges, passing trains, and the condition of the rails, but he must act at the same moment, working throttle, air brakes, or reversing lever ... for there is no time to think."

Self-discipline and an intuitive "sixth sense," the article noted, were also vital to an engineer's survival. At sixty miles per hour, a train traveled about ninety feet in a second. With the monotony of running the same route day after day, there was always the chance that the engineer might forget the location of a switch and run off the track, or fail to see an obstacle on the track ahead.

Clearly, extraordinary skills were required to be an engineer, the popular "hero of the rails," at the turn of the century. The title was well justified—the man who sat on the right side of the cab performed his duties in the most dangerous part of the train. He was in charge of a massive, hurtling piece of machinery equipped with a steam boiler that could instantly explode.

Archie Buchanan described more about was expected of the engine driver:

> He must know his engine like a book, backward and forward, must know how to manage her when she is sick and well, and what to do if an eccentric breaks or a piston gets leaking or a valve spindle is bent. He must know how to work the injector so as to keep water enough in the boiler without wasting any by the steam blowing off. He must be able to save power by working the steam expansively and yet keeping up his speed; he must know every inch of the road, the grades, bridges, switches, curves, and tunnels, and all the trains he has to pass or which may pass him. He must be able to control his train and engine at full speed, must understand the effect of the weather on the rails, must know how to use the air brakes and the reversing lever, and when not to use them.

If Henry ever read Buchanan's comments in *McClure's*, they certainly didn't deter him from his goal. He had a decade of experience firing engines and was ready and eager to make the transition to the right side of the cab. In the spring of 1898, a time when many Schenectady men were rallying to the cry "Remember the Maine and to hell with Spain," Henry put in his application for an engineer's position.

Career paths on the railroad were governed by a strict seniority system, which often resulted in firemen working ten years or more before they were eligible for promotion.[3] The New York Central's qualifications were likely similar to those of its rival, the Pennsylvania Railroad. Applicants had to be at least twenty-one years of age, have enough education to fill out an application, pass a simple reading test, and be in excellent physical condition. Beyond this, technical knowledge of engines, a skill learned only from experience, was a distinct plus.[4]

Some railroads had stiffer requirements than the Pennsy. An applicant could be scrutinized for his knowledge of train rules, signal rules, and operating procedures. Henry, for example, could be quizzed about the main features of the Central's four-track system—the location of signals, curves, and changes in grade over the route in the railroad's Mohawk Division.

Most of the men in engineers' jobs were native born, white, and Protestant. Railroads often gave preference to men of Irish or English origin.[5] It was also a time when relations between America and Germany were strained, mostly because of trade disputes and German rivalry in the Spanish-American War. In fact, the German Ambassador in Washington reported that his was the country most hated by Americans.[6] Many German-Americans decided to "Americanize" their surnames. Henry was no exception; he began spelling his family's name the American way, with a single "n"—Horstman.

The New York Central's man in charge of promotions (probably the master mechanic) was no doubt aware that Henry was the nephew of the deceased Friedrich Horstmann who enjoyed a sterling professional reputation during his long career with the railroad. Better yet, Henry possessed the qualities railroad bosses sought for the all-important job of running their trains—a calm demeanor, physical strength, technical skill, and a demonstrated ability to follow orders.

Finally, after nearly a decade of shoveling coal into the ravenous boilers that powered the Central's locomotives,

Henry Horstman was promoted to an engineer's position. His boyhood dream was realized as he joined the ranks of an elite class of railroad men, sometimes called "hoggers," who enjoyed prestige within their companies and in the communities where they lived. And his new status allowed him to join one of the most powerful unions in the nation, the Brotherhood of Locomotive Engineers (BLE).

After struggling through the seemingly endless economic depression, it was a joyous occasion at 22 Mynderse Street when Henry brought home news of his promotion. His move up the ranks meant not only better pay, but relief from the dirty, backbreaking fireman's job. The usual starting pay for a new engineer was about $100 a month. A freight train engineer with regular assignments could make as much as $150 a month, more than double the $60 a month firemen were paid. Passenger train engineers, the highest paid trainmen, could earn up to $175 a month.[7]

Henry's enthusiasm for his new assignment was tempered with reality. His growing family was dependent on him. The railroad made it clear that its employees assumed all risks related to their jobs. What would his family do if he was injured or, worse yet, killed on the job? The loss of income from such a disaster was a trainman's greatest fear. Many engineers purchased life insurance from the BLE. But Henry's first purchase was a cemetery plot in the German section of Schenectady's Vale cemetery. He paid $37 for a lot just a few yards away from the gravesite of his uncle Friedrich, laid to rest there seven years earlier.[8]

The newly promoted engineer likely spent some time running a switcher, a workhorse engine that pulled cars back and forth to make up trams (trolleys and street cars) in the West Albany Yard. At some point, probably within a year, Henry was cleared to run freight trains, the backbone of the railroad's business. But unlike the Central's senior engineers, new enginemen couldn't rely on steady work and income. Junior enginemen were assigned to irregular runs and their earnings could fluctuate wildly.[9]

A freight engineer's workdays were dominated by demands to get his trains from one point to another, and to do it by the books. This usually meant at least ten hours a day riding the rails with only occasional days off. Sometimes he was gone from home for two or three days at a stretch. These long hours required him to keep up with schedules designed by the railroad not for humans, but for moving goods to market. Irregular schedules created fatigued train crews in the 24/7 railroad business. It was work that provided little relief from physical and mental exhaustion.

Engineer Henry Horstman at Mynderse Street house, ca. 1900. On wall is photo of his father in Hille, Christian Friedrich Horstmann.

The engineer's job had undergone many changes since his uncle's time. Gone was the earlier practice whereby an engineer assigned to a single locomotive was responsible for its maintenance, frills, and decorations. Now the Central pooled its growing fleet of engines so that engineers ran whatever locomotive was available on a given day. Under this system, freight engineers took their assignments on a pool basis, with all men in the pool operating on a first-in, first-out basis. Although an engineer no longer had his own engine, he handled a more powerful locomotive that pulled a heavier load at a faster speed.

Running a freight train was a much different job than heading up a fast passenger train tied to a rigid schedule. The freight engineer focused his attention on getting the maximum amount of power out of his engine while using the minimum amount of fuel, rather than getting to a scheduled stop on time. One who wasted time and fuel risked a scathing reception from the master mechanic when he returned from his run. And unlike the faster passenger trains, many freight trains were not equipped with air brakes.

The newly designed engines coming on line were a quantum leap from their smaller, slower predecessors. Designers like William Buchanan created engines that could accomplish the same work with one engine and one crew that was previously done with two engines and two engineers. By 1900, powerful new freight locomotives that could deliver up to 1,500 horsepower allowed the railroads to double their average trainloads. Longer, heavier and faster trains pulled by more powerful engines meant more profit for the railroads.[10]

The longer trains, some with as many as eighty freight cars, caused work hours to escalate. At the same time, sharp increases in the weight of freight cars increased the danger of rail and wheel failures.[11] Railroad managers drove men and equipment to the breaking point, demanding that workers ignore their body clocks and adapt to schedules designed to keep goods moving on the rails. Their goal was to keep the traffic moving and in doing so, they produced too many sleep-deprived trainmen. It was a workplace environment guaranteed to produce casualties.

Soaring railroad accident rates after 1897 produced a steady run of sensational newspaper stories with titles like "Railway Massacres."[12] Still, railroads like the New York Central fought tooth and nail to prevent any regulation of the rates they charged or on the way they conducted their rail operations. When it came to safety, the railroads not only delayed implementation of the 1893 Appliance Safety Act but they blocked numerous proposals in the U.S. Congress for new laws requiring automatic block signals, accident investigations, and locomotive inspections.

The railroads adamantly opposed legislation to address the issue of fatigue caused by the long working hours they imposed on their trainmen. The lack of protection for trainmen from demands by employers to work unlimited hours was just one of many indignities. Men who rode the rails received no compensation for on-the-job injuries, no retirement pensions, and no unemployment compensation.

The railroads also fought attempts in Congress to require restitution for employees injured or killed on the job. Liability laws of the day made accidents cheap for railroads so they had no interest in revising what would quickly drive up their costs.[13] Instead, they put their financial weight behind political bosses who returned the favor by sending railroad-friendly men to Congress.

In a nutshell, the railroads were prepared to do whatever it would take to prevent the federal government from interfering with their businesses. The New York Central's president, Chauncey Depew, was the proverbial "fox in the chicken coop." Always enamored with politics, Depew simultaneously served in the United States Senate while he was chairman of the powerful New York Central and Hudson River Railroad. It was a blatant conflict of interest that would compromise the safety of thousands of trainmen, including Henry Horstman.

Ten

THE RAILROAD SENATOR

*Of all the creatures of the Vanderbilts, none has been more versatile,
more willing, or more profitable to his users than Depew.*

David Graham Phillips, *The Treason of the Senate*, March 1906.

"*Mr. Depew for the Senate*" proclaimed a headline in the *New York Times* on November 15, 1898. The story reported that the New York Central's well-known president was endorsed by Senator Thomas Platt, the New York State Republican party boss, to be the party's candidate for the United States Senate.

Henry and his fellow Central engineers were surely not surprised by the news, given Depew's previous attempts to run for public office. Earlier that year, about the time Henry was promoted, the railroad's president had quietly let it be known that he was interested in running for the seat of retiring Senator Edward Murphy. Rumors circulated that the Vanderbilts (brothers Cornelius II, Willie, and Frederick were directors of the Central) ordered Senator Platt to name Depew as the party's choice.

Along with his prominence as a railroad chief, Depew had a reputation as a superb orator. He composed speeches in his head as a form of relaxation and perfected a casual, witty speaking style. As the company's principal spokesman, he appeared before groups around the country, sometimes five nights a week, ostensibly to help burnish the railroad's public image. He became a widely sought orator and was so good at it that he was chosen to speak at numerous public events including the opening of the World's Fair in Chicago in 1893. He delivered nominating speeches at Republican conventions in 1888 and 1896. The *New York Times* gushed that Depew was "a philosopher, and one of the wise men of the Western world."[1]

An introduction to a book of Depew's speeches described Depew as "probably the best known American living today, with the sole exception of the President of the United States." It continued, "the name of Edison has penetrated to remoter corners of the globe than that of Depew, but it would hardly be claimed that the personality of the great inventor is familiar to half so many men." The Central's president, the review suggested, "is almost as accessible to the employees of his Company as he is to its Directors—as accessible as he is to the reporters who daily haunt his office, and to whom he unbosoms himself with freedom …"[2]

Not a traditional railroad man, Depew thrived in the political world. His skills as a lawyer and lobbyist were invaluable to the Vanderbilts, who were under constant attack from public officials. These were talents that led to his rise to the presidency of the railroad. Yet his ascendancy at the Central occurred during a time when railroads were at the center of political corruption. Their deceit and dishonesty covered the gamut of illegal activity and unethical conduct, ranging from outright bribes to free transportation for politicians, and it existed at all levels of government.

The prevailing attitude was bluntly put by Collis P. Huntington, a founder of the Central Pacific Railroad: "If you have to pay money (to a politician) to have the right thing done, it is only just and fair to do it.… If a politician has the power to do great evil and won't do right unless he is bribed to do it, I think … it is a man's duty to go up and bribe him."[3]

ALFRED
HENRY
LEWIS,
Editor.

THE VERDICT

PRICE,
TEN
CENTS.

VOL. I.   NEW YORK, (⸻) JANUARY 16, 1899.   NO. 5.

MIRS

MY MASTER'S CHAIR.

NEW YORK CENTRAL

TRUSTS MONOPOLY

Magazine cover depicting New York's "Independent and
Unfettered" U.S. Senator (U.S. Library of Congress)

Chauncey Depew was no stranger to these tactics. He was
Commodore Vanderbilt's lawyer during the notorious "Battle of the

Bribes," when Vanderbilt prevailed by greasing the palms of more legislators than his archenemy, the so-called "Erie Ring" of railrogues— Daniel Drew, Jay Gould, and Jim Fisk.[4]

The Vanderbilts put Depew's legal and political skills to good use as they assembled their railroad empire. From his first post in Albany, the state capital, Depew lobbied to prevent regulation and taxation of the company.[5] The Commodore and his son amassed enormous personal wealth from deals Depew struck with the state legislators. Permission from the legislature to consolidate several railways gave the Vanderbilts free grants of franchises worth hundreds of millions of dollars.

As the Vanderbilt railroad empire grew to dominate the eastern United States, William H. Vanderbilt's monopolistic practices made him one of the most hated men in America. He relied heavily on Depew to deal with politicians and the public. On one occasion, when a bill to relieve the New York Central from payment of judgments in pending suits against it and to allow the railroad to raise its passenger fares was defeated, Depew had it resurrected, hidden in another bill, and passed.[6] "During that hour, Depew was the busiest man in the lobby," observed the *Buffalo Express*. Another Buffalo newspaper was not so generous: "Depew stands convicted of being a corrupter of the lawmakers of the commonwealth," it charged.

Another tactic Depew used was to pull out all the stops to kill a bill that threatened the Central's interests and then, if its passage appeared likely, he would support a weaker backup version. When the state legislature was about to pass a bill giving the state authority to regulate railroad shipping rates, Depew threw his weight behind a scaled down version that included a less radical and relatively toothless railroad commission. His version passed.[7]

Depew was the undisputed king of the railroad industry's influence peddlers. A master lobbyist, he knew all the tricks of his trade. One of his favorite devices was the "railroad free pass," a particularly effective political inducement to win a legislator's support.

Depew was "the most magnificent bestower of passes in all history," wrote Mark Sullivan, a chronicler of the times, who dubbed him "The Ambassador of Legislation and Politics."[8] Sullivan explained how the free pass was used by the canny Depew and his fellow railroad lobbyists:

> In each State, as the first of every January approached, the railroads sent annual passes to the Governor and all state officials, to all the members of the legislature and, especially, to the heads and leaders of the two party organizations; in every community they delivered passes to the county or municipal officials, to the local officials of the two party organizations, to the newspaper editors, to practically every person in a position to influence either legislation, court decision, administrative action, or public opinion.

Not surprisingly, public officials and others who managed to finagle a free pass considered it an honor, not a bribe. Being able to "flash a pass" on the railroad was a mark of someone who held influence and power. "Men of high degree who would look with horror upon a direct bribe were as eager for passes as a dipsomaniac for drink," Sullivan observed.[9]

Legislators or party leaders could get passes for constituents or the party faithful by applying to a railroad for a "trip pass." Political leaders and bosses obtained free passes for delegates to state conventions. Ministers and community leaders received free passes in return for their support.

Newspapermen, too, were frequent recipients of free passes. The Pennsylvania Railroad, the New York Central's arch rival, was so generous to media men in Washington that one reporter remarked: "So far as I am concerned, if the Pennsylvania Railroad wants the Capitol Rotunda for a roundhouse they can have it."[10]

Pity the railroad that denied a free pass request to a newsman. When William H. Vanderbilt turned down a newspaper publisher's request for an annual pass, the irate applicant threatened to publish a picture of wrecked railroad cars on fire with headless, bleeding bodies and baggage spread across the scene. "Killed and Wounded on the New York Central Railroad," charged its caption. A picture of the bewhiskered Vanderbilt, "Owner of the Road," was accompanied by a row of coffins listing all the Central's previous accidents. Vanderbilt relented; the man got his passes, and the picture was never published.

Revelations about Depew's free passes sparked comments in newspapers around the state, causing the Olean, New York *Weekly Democrat* to observe that the handouts give the railroads "a power over the state legislature that is difficult to overcome ... and enable them to become tax-dodgers ..."[11]

No doubt, Depew was embarrassed when the *New York World* made public a batch of letters from public officials begging him for free passes. Among them was a long list of tax assessors who sought favors "on the express grounds that they keep the assessments of the railroad corporation down and cheat the honest taxpayers of the state." One assessor's letter asked for (and received) free passes for himself and his two sons. "I hope under the circumstances you are pleased with your assessment this year," the man wrote.

It was no surprise to find politicians soliciting Mr. Depew for tickets, the *World* chortled, citing one senator who sought passes for himself and five members of his family from Syracuse to Kansas City and return. Another begged passes for a relative and two little daughters, reminding Mr. Depew "that it would save him much trouble and a little cash if his season ticket should be renewed."

Yet Depew didn't comply with every request. When an out-of-favor New York City politician solicited him for a free pass to Chicago, the sharp-witted lobbyist replied he couldn't provide the return trip but would be more than happy to give him a one-way pass to Chicago "or to any more distant city."[12]

Not that he was a man who couldn't show compassion. On one occasion, Depew and J.P. Morgan were traveling in a special train to Boston on a rainy night. When their speeding train hit something on the track, Depew ordered the train to stop and return to the scene where he found "a poor fellow lying there dead, crushed like a worm."[13]

Learning that the man who was run down in the dark had a wife and two children, he reportedly said to his traveling companions, "Now, gentlemen, I wish to make a collection for the poor fellow's family ... something that will smooth the rough way that his hapless widow and children will have to tread. I will lead the list with $100."

Corruption spawned by the railroad free passes was so rampant that the *Philadelphia North American* proclaimed "there is really no exaggeration in the assertion that no single influence has done so much to poison the very fountain of political life as the railroad free pass"[14] (Congress banned the practice in 1906).

Depew's widespread recognition helped launch his attempt to win the Republican nomination for president in 1888, the year when Henry became a fireman on the Central. Later Depew claimed in his biography that he made no effort to win the nomination. It was "against my published wishes" he wrote, that he was presented as New York's candidate for president "with unprecedented unanimity."[15] He attributed his withdrawal from that race to "the intense hostility of railroad men in the Western States."

A decade later, Depew openly pursued the New York seat in the United States Senate, a position he had coveted since he was first hired by Commodore Vanderbilt who persuaded him that he would be a "damned fool" if he didn't choose railroads over politics as a career. Depew later said he took the job because Vanderbilt's railroad "may grow and if it does, I will grow with it. If I then want to go to the Senate or get a mission when I am old, I can get it."[16]

Depew achieved his long-sought ambition in January 1899 when New York's Republican-controlled state legislature elected him to that position (U.S. Senators weren't elected by voters until 1913). Later in the year, the sixty-five-year-old Depew retired from the Central's presidency and replaced the ailing Cornelius Vanderbilt II as chairman of the railroad's board of directors, a position that gave him oversight over all aspects of the giant railroad's twenty-two-thousand-mile system.

The newly elected senator had no intention of relinquishing his position as chairman of the railroad. Depew recognized that as a senator he could help block or kill proposals that adversely impacted the New York Central. Although holding both positions simultaneously apparently didn't violate any existing laws, the blatant conflict of interest helped fuel public demands for Congress to rein in the mighty railroads. It was as if today's chairman of ExxonMobil served simultaneously in the U.S. Senate.

Mindful of the criticism, the newly elected senator moved quickly to assure railroad workers that he would protect them from the "evil effect" of unwise railroad legislation. On February 24, 1899, one week before he took office, he addressed a standing-room-only crowd at a meeting of the Congress of Railway Employees in Chicago: "Legislators and public men do not mean to do injustice, except a few demagogues. The rest are honest minded to do what is right."[17]

"If I may be personal," he continued, "the best evidence of the disappearance of the railway question (i.e., government ownership) from our politics and of the people of the Empire State that a man engaged in the railway business is doing his part as honestly as any other (citizen) ... is my election this winter to the United States Senate." But by the time Senator Depew began his second (and last) term in the Senate in 1906 his self-description as an honest citizen would ring hollow.

Perhaps engineer Horstman and his fellow trainmen on the New York Central believed they could count on Senator Depew to support their interests in Congress when it came to protecting them from the widely publicized hazards of their work. In New York State alone, more than 2,645 railroad accidents in 1900 took the lives of 671 persons (railroad workers and passengers), while another 1,374 were injured.[18] But as the saying goes, a man cannot serve two masters. Senator Depew's indisputable "master" was not the New York Central's trainmen, its customers, or even the people of New York State. His allegiance was to the Vanderbilt interests.

At the dawn of the twentieth century, the Central's board of directors included Senator Depew and J.P. Morgan, the "Dictator of Wall Street." Morgan's investments in numerous railroads gave him the power to choose their managers, dictate their policies, and shape them to his principles (by 1902 he had control over five thousand miles of American railroads).[19] Neither Depew nor Morgan showed any interest in improving railroad safety, even as casualties on the rails grew to unprecedented levels. Neither did Willie K. Vanderbilt and other Vanderbilt directors of the Central—their interest in the railroad steadily diminished as they found new ways to spend their inherited wealth.[20]

From their lofty perspectives, the men who sat atop the railroad viewed government regulation as the enemy—no matter whether it was designed to set railroad rates or to save their workers' lives. They were the imperious, egotistical champions of "America's Greatest Railroad," who venerated profits and machines over the men who rode the rails.

In April 1903, Schenectady's *Das Deutsche Journal*, a German-language weekly newspaper published by a German-American, cogently concluded that "the rise of the few always happens on the backs of the many."[21] Few men provided better examples than the directors of the New York Central and Hudson River Railroad.

Eleven

IN THE SHADOW OF CASEY JONES

The strain, both mental and physical, on those who are engaged in the movement and operation of railroad trains under modern conditions is perhaps greater than that which exists in any other industry.

President Teddy Roosevelt in a message to Congress, 1905

By the turn of the century, nearly every city and town in America was connected to a railroad. Five transcontinental routes and more than 210,000 miles of track blanketed the nation like a spider web. Profits rose as the railroads reduced rates and put powerful locomotives that pulled longer, heavier and faster trains into service. It was the beginning of a "Golden Age" of railroading.

In 1900, the railroads were the nation's largest employer with more than a million workers. The New York Central itself employed more than twenty-two thousand while operating a fleet of more than one thousand locomotives.[1] In New York State some 9,508 engineers and firemen worked for steam railroads. Henry was one of 313 railroad workers who lived in Schenectady and most of them were Central employees.[2]

A lead story in the *Saturday Evening Post*, "The Making of a Railroad Man," featured William J. McQueen, a veteran New York Central engineman.[3] McQueen painted a bright future for those who earned a coveted engineer's position: "Work is plenty, pay is good, and the demand for experienced and reliable men has never been greater," he wrote. Still, McQueen couldn't ignore the dangers of his job. He candidly recounted an incident that nearly took his life when he was driving the Central's *Eastern Express*:

> Coming down from Albany one night, I had almost reached Hyde Park when I saw ahead of me a freight conductor signaling with his lantern. He was near a switch and I supposed he was communicating with his own crew. It flashed across my mind that something was wrong and I instantly put on the brake, shut off the steam, reversed, and sanded the track. We were running at the rate of fifty mph, but before we reached the switch, we had slowed down to thirty. Some cars had been derailed and tipped over on our track, and these we struck with such force that our engine, express and mail cars left the rails and plunged into the Hudson River. When we reached the bottom, the water was five to six feet over my head. I tried to crawl out of the cab but was wedged in so that I could not move. I was just giving myself up for lost when I heard something give way about the boiler and the engine partly turned over and released me. I shot up to the surface thoroughly exhausted, nearly unconscious, but otherwise uninjured. The fireman had come up as soon as the engine touched bottom.

McQueen's story was just one of many life-threatening incidents on the rails that helped create a glamorous image of the railroad engineer at work in a dangerous environment. His account was quickly surpassed by an accident that triggered the most famous railroad legend of all time.

On April 30, 1900, Illinois Central engineer John Luther "Casey" Jones was at the helm of the *Cannonball Express* when his train plowed into a stalled freight near Vaughan, Mississippi. Newspapers across the nation ran headlines about the brave engineer who stayed at the throttle and sacrificed his life in order to save his passengers.[4]

Casey, who coincidentally was born in the same year as Henry, was soon immortalized in songs and books, his legend becoming part of American folklore. By 1902, a song about him ranked among the top ten that year, and it eventually morphed into "The Ballad of Casey Jones":

> *Come all you rounders, I want you to hear*
> *The story told of a brave engineer.*
> *Casey Jones was the rounder's name;*
> *On a six-eight wheeler, boys, he won his fame.*
> *Now the caller called Casey 'bout half-past four;*
> *He kissed his wife at the station door,*
> *He mounted to the cab with his orders in hand,*
> *Said, "I'm gonna take my trip to the Promised Land."[5]*

But the facts surrounding the fast-growing legend didn't add up. As it happened, the accident was Casey's own fault—the engineer was "highballing" (running too fast) when his locomotive slammed into the caboose of the freight train. As one railroad historian puts it: "The not-so-accurate story of a not-so-heroic engineer involved in a not-so-important accident captured the popular imagination."[6] Yet Casey's fame lent a lasting glamour to his profession even though it didn't square with the facts.

By 1901, demands for an accurate accounting of casualties on the nation's railways reached the U.S. Congress. The Accident Reports Act was the first railroad safety bill to be considered since Senator Depew's arrival there in 1899. It required railroads to make full monthly reports to the ICC of all train accidents involving injuries to employees and passengers. The reports were to be backed by sworn statements from each railroad. A railroad failing to make a report within thirty days of the end of a month was guilty of a misdemeanor.

Despite the bill's logic, the railroads set out to kill it. Railroad-friendly senators enlisted Edward Wolcott, a senator who had just lost his reelection bid, to do their handiwork. Wolcott declared the bill was "useless legislation" designed merely to give the ICC something to do. "The railroad business is the safest in the world," he blustered, "no human lives would be saved by passing a bill like this ... tell us how dangerous the ocean is: would ships sail with far greater safety if [we] had an account of all the drownings that take place in the world?"[7]

Senator Wolcott directed blame for railroad casualties at the trainmen themselves who, he claimed, were responsible "for 95 percent of all casualties." These men were not injured "by the character of railroad directors," he suggested, but by "the negligence of some brother employee who does not mean to do so."

During the debate, Senator Depew's renowned oratorical skills were absent. He was uncharacteristically silent and offered no comment, failing to speak up for trainmen who risked life and limb every day. In the end, senators who supported the bill managed to muster enough votes to call Senator Wolcott's bluff. The legislation passed by voice vote, a practice that shields senators from publicly disclosing their votes.

The Accident Reports Act became law in 1901. In the three years that followed, the reports produced by the ICC provided sobering and incontrovertible evidence of the carnage on the railways. The ICC's annual report in 1904 grimly detailed what it called "the risks of railroad travel and the dangers pertaining to the everyday life of railroad employees":[8]

(Years ending June 30)			
	1902	1903	1904
Employees injured	33,711	39,004	43,266
Employees killed	2,516	3,233	3,367
Passengers injured	6,089	6,973	8,077
Passengers killed	303	321	420
Total killed and injured:	42,619	49,531	55,130

The ICC reports demonstrated that although spectacular accidents attracted the most media attention, it was the trainmen—the enginemen, firemen, brakemen, and conductors working on trains—who bore the brunt of the carnage (see table below). Most of the casualties were the result of unspectacular "little" accidents that resulted from coupling and uncoupling cars, falling off trains, or striking obstructions along the road or in the rail yards, where clearances were too tight. It was these "little accidents" that caused most of the killing and maiming, writes Mark Aldrich, author of *Death Rode the Rails*.[9]

(Years ending June 30)

	1902		1903		1904	
	Killed	Injured	Killed	Injured	Killed	Injured
Train accidents	697	5,046	895	6,440	844	6,990
Coupling accidents	143	2,113	253	2,788	278	3,441
Overhead obstructions	104	1,070	93	992	116	1,210
Falling from cars	537	6,867	678	8,025	700	9,371
Other causes	1,035	18,615	1,314	20,759	1,429	22,254
Total Employees:	2,516	33,711	3,233	39,004	3,367	43,266

Casualty claims regularly published in the *Railroad Trainmen's Journal* provided gruesome evidence of the carnage. Typical were these "beneficiary assessment notices" issued for trainmen in February 1903:[10]

- Fell from engine; run over. $1,200.
- Struck by overhead bridge. $1,200.
- Fell between cars while switching, run over. $ 800.
- Thrown from train, left leg run over, amputated. $1,200.
- Right hand crushed while coupling; amputated. $1,200.

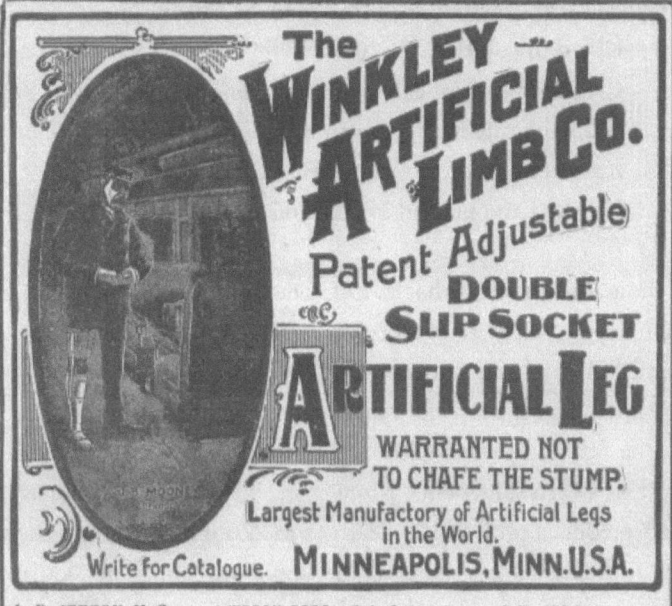
Advertisement for artificial limbs with testimonials from trainmen (*Railroad Trainmen's Journal*, January 1903).

- Struck by engine. $ 400.
- Fell from engine; skull fractured. $1,200.
- Killed in collision. $1,200
- Crushed between cars while adjusting coupler. $ 400.
- Fell from car; both legs run over; amputated. $1,200.
- Knocked from train; run over. $1,200.
- Crushed and burned in collision. $ 800.

The awful truth was that in 1903 one trainman was killed for every 123 employed, while one of every ten was injured, according to the ICC. In fact, these frightful statistics didn't tell the whole story. The agency complained that it received many inaccurate and incomplete reports from the railroads, some with deaths and injuries "entirely omitted" from their sworn statements. More than sixty railroads admitted they failed to report a total of 109 deaths and 226 injuries during the year. Many railroads simply ignored the law even though it required all accidents to be reported under oath.[11]

Despite the daunting casualty figures, men who ran the trains still believed they had the "most glamorous job on earth."[12] Engineers were among the best-paid workmen of the time and many, like Henry, could afford to own houses and raise families. The reality of working on the railroad, one chronicler of railroad history suggests, seldom disappointed those who were lucky enough to survive it.[13]

On June 15, 1902, the New York Central launched the *Twentieth Century Limited*, billed by the railroad as "the fastest long distance train in the world."[14] On its first run, the sleek new train covered the 980 miles between New York and Chicago in 20 hours, or as one passenger exclaimed, "like a bat out of hell."[15] Designed for travelers who demanded both speed and luxury, it boasted three luxurious Pullman sleeper cars, a buffet, and a diner. Its elaborate furnishings even included electric lights. To pamper its passengers, the train provided a barber shop, a maid, a valet, and a stenographer.

The *Twentieth Century Limited* instantly became a household name throughout America, a striking symbol of the glamour associated with a "Golden Age" of railroading. Every engineer's dream was to be at the controls of a locomotive that headed up a train like the *Twentieth Century Limited*.

But in reality, the train's flashy title was an unintended warning for the intrepid men who ran the rails.

New York Central's **Twentieth Century Limited**, "the fastest long distance train in the world"(old postcard).

Twelve

A DREAM DERAILED

*Train accidents were actually only a small part of the railroad
safety problem. Most casualties resulted from "little accidents"
… Like sniping, they picked off victims one at a time.*

Mark Aldrich, *Death Rode the Rails*[1]

Henry and Louisa Horstman had plenty of reasons to be optimistic as they waited for the turn of the century on New Year's Eve, 1899.

For one, they anticipated the birth of their fourth child within a few days. Prospects for Henry, who was living his boyhood dream, had never been brighter. He looked forward to the day when he could move up to passenger trains. A promotion would mean more predictable hours, a higher pay scale, and more time to be with his growing family.

On the third day of the new century, Louisa gave birth to a healthy baby boy. Like his siblings, Raymond was born in the Mynderse Street house (95 percent of all births in the United States in 1900 took place in the home). But within a few days of Raymond's arrival, the joyous occasion was dampened when nine-year-old Jessie complained of a severe pain in her abdomen. As Jessie's pain worsened and her fever rose, her parents probably called in a neighbor, Dr. Janet Murray,

Schenectady's first female physician, who lived just a few doors away on Mynderse Street.

Jessie had contracted appendicitis, an illness for which there was no effective treatment. Antibiotics had yet to be invented and surgery to remove an appendix was only in its infancy. The standard treatment of the time was to drain the abscess, a procedure which was probably performed at the city's Ellis Hospital, located then on Jay Street next to City Hall. But when Jessie's appendix burst, nothing could be done to save her.

The loss of their first child was a hard blow to the young couple at a time when their future seemed secure and promising. No doubt Jessie's death brought back memories of siblings in the "Old Country" whose lives were also taken suddenly by mysterious, untreatable illnesses. The grieving couple buried their daughter in the plot Henry had purchased in the city's Vale cemetery. In America, one of every four children born would not live to celebrate their eighteenth birthday. And Jessie would not be the last of the Horstman *kinder* to be included in that unforgiving statistic.

By the turn of the century, Schenectady's population had swelled to 31,682 from a pre-depression count of 22,858 in 1892.[2] The city's growth was evidence that it was spared from the worst of the "Cleveland depression." Its booming economy was led by the fast-growing General Electric Company while the Big Shop, bursting with orders for the iron horses that fueled the nation's growth, merged in 1901 with seven other locomotive builders to form the American Locomotive Company.

A tide of visiting businessmen kept the Edison Hotel at capacity. New houses were under construction along the trolley lines that spread out from the city. The German-language newspaper, *Das Deutsche Journal*, was named one of two official city newspapers. The Van Curler Opera House attracted large crowds of theatergoers. Ladies in wide-brimmed hats with ostrich feathers shopped at Barney's Department store and bought groceries at Flinn's market, where five pounds of beans cost twenty-five cents, bacon eighteen cents a pound, and hamburger steaks sold two for twenty-five cents.[3]

Henry and Louisa Horstman

Jessie Horstman

Of course, life had to go on in the Horstman household. The family needed to be fed and clothed—a challenging task for Louisa with Henry gone, often many days at a stretch, and his income little more than four dollars a day.[4] Spouses of Central engineers who lived in the city shared a common bond not unlike that of wives whose husbands go off to war. They kept a constant eye on newspapers for reports of men who had been injured or killed on the job.

In the summer of 1902, Louisa gave birth to another healthy boy, Elmer. The four children slept two to a room in the cramped Horstman household, with the two youngest occupying their parents' bedroom. The oldest children, Clarence and Irene, attended nearby Halsey School, sometimes called the Albany Street School.

To help make ends meet, Henry rented the upstairs portion of the house to Henry Bartling, another German-born engineman on the Central and a fellow member of the BLE's Division #172 in Schenectady. It was a good arrangement; the two men could travel to work together and share information about conditions on the line and a myriad of technical details about engine running.

Henry was captivated by the high speed engines rolling off the assembly lines at the "Big Shop" in Schenectady. A ten-wheeler designed by William Buchanan was the Concorde of its time and pulled trains like the *Empire State Express*. But the reality was that only the most senior and highly skilled engineers got those plum assignments. Henry likely needed at least five more years of experience before he could qualify for passenger service. And it could be many years after that before he earned the right to head up a fast express. Undeterred, Henry knew that his uncle had risen through the ranks to drive the fastest trains of his day. The resolute immigrant had every intention of following in Friedrich Horstmann's footsteps.

Henry prized a photo of this 4-6-0 Class F-3a locomotive built in Schenectady. (Courtesy of New York Central System Historical Society)

Engineers, by their nature, were a close-knit group. Word about accidents traveled swiftly through their ranks—where an accident occurred; who was injured or killed; and who was disciplined by the railroad's hard-driving managers. In the first eight months of 1903, many serious mishaps occurred on the Central's system.[5] Among the most severe were these:

- **Castleton, New York, January.** A boiler explosion on a freight train near Castleton blew the engineman and fireman from the locomotive, killing them both.
- **Fulton, New York, April.** A head-on collision between passenger trains at Fulton resulted in multiple injuries to both passengers and crew.
- **Hoffmans, New York, April.** A freight train ran into a milk train. One worker was killed and five others injured.
- **Nelson, New York, May.** A head-on collision at a siding resulted in a fireman and conductor being killed. And in June, a locomotive dropped its crown sheet, killing a fireman and scalding a brakeman.
- **Little Falls, New York, August.** A fast newspaper train

derailed on the Gulf Curve, killing the engineer and fireman, and leaving many others with serious injuries.

- **Oneida, New York, August.** Two freight trains collided, injuring both the brakeman and conductor.
- **Brewster, New York, August.** A head-on collision between a passenger train and a freight train killed a fireman.

Still more unwelcome news surfaced in July when the BLE's Grand Chief Engineer, P.M Arthur, a leader in the struggle to improve working conditions for engineers, collapsed and died in the midst of a speech he was giving to Canadian engineers.[6]

Of course, accidents weren't confined to the New York Central. On September 27, it was the Southern Railway's *Fast Mail* ("Old 97") that failed to negotiate a curve, leaped the rails, and plunged one hundred feet into the river. Two firemen, the conductor, a flagman, and eight others aboard the ill-fated train were killed. The engineer was found in the wreck "with his hand on the throttle, a-scalded to death with steam."[7]

Like most railroads, the Central's demand for engineers and rail crews was at a high level in 1903. Freight engineers were told to keep freight moving at all costs; increasing the line's tonnage was the name of the game. Henry worked every shift he could get, logging many long, hard hours. A crew could be on a job for twenty-four hours without a break or work two long shifts with only a few hours rest. For Henry, whose family included two infants (Elmer and Raymond), getting badly needed rest at home was often impossible. Long hours riding the rails and little rest in between assignments were a prescription for disaster in an occupation that yielded no margin for error.

Less than a week after the well-publicized wreck of "Old 97," Henry took an assignment normally relegated to rookie engineers. He may have volunteered for the job or it was randomly assigned to him. Whatever the case, his task was to drive a local freight known as a "pickup," so named because it delivered and picked up produce at stops all along the line. In central New York State, these trains were the lifelines of the small towns and villages strung along the Mohawk Valley with their mills, dairies, breweries, canneries, and factories.

Running a pickup was not a plum assignment and a far cry from Henry's ambition to drive advanced-design locomotives like the 4-6-0 speedsters designed by the Central's William Buchanan. On this October day, Henry's pickup was headed up by New York Central's locomotive No. 663, an outmoded engine that had little resemblance to the new high-tech marvels.[8] His train orders directed him to return the locomotive to West Albany for repairs after his run was completed.

Pickups traveled at slow speeds on the Central's freight tracks, sometimes with as many as sixty cars. Maneuvering in and out of sidings and freight yards located like spider webs over the Central's four-track system, they had to stay out of the way of faster freight trains. Susceptible to delays and mechanical breakdowns, they often spent more time on sidings and in rail yards than on the main line. For the pickup's crew, it was hard, not-so-glamorous duty that could easily double a twelve-hour day and require an overnight stay along the way.

Henry's run likely began in Carmen, a railroad junction on the outskirts of Schenectady where the Central operated a freight depot.[9] His engine steamed out of Carmen, the train swinging and swaying as it made its way past an array of signals and headed west on track 3 of the Central's "water level route," the practically gradeless main line that connected New York City and Buffalo. The Central's four-track system was the throbbing, main aorta of rail service in the northeastern United States. Between Albany and Buffalo, tracks were numbered from the south so that tracks #2 and #1 were reserved for passenger trains (east- and westbound) while tracks #3 and #4 were designated for freight traffic (west- and eastbound).

Even though the water level route was flat, it was not straight as it followed the Mohawk River across the Empire State. Henry had traveled the route many times before, both as a fireman and a freight engineer, and he was certainly well acquainted with its bends, dips and turns, road crossings, bridges, sidings, and stations.

Running the pickup's route was taxing work as he continued west. Despite the train's plodding pace, there was no opportunity to relax and enjoy the spectacular fall scenery of the Mohawk valley. Freight cars behind him had to be visually checked for overheated "hotboxes" (bearings). He had to lean out of the cab to get signals from his brakeman, or stand on the gangway to watch down the tracks for other trains. The train had to be stopped to take on water or coal, and maneuver on and off sidings to drop off or pick up cars. Then, too, the plodding pickups were prime targets for "open-air navigators" to hitch a ride.

Henry's heavily laden pickup made stops at sidings and yards in villages and towns along the Mohawk: Amsterdam, Tribes Hill, Fonda, Fort Plain, Little Falls, Herkimer, Ilion, Utica, and Rome. It's not clear when or where his train reached the last stop on its outgoing run. Delays could have required an overnight stay for the crew at Rome, some ninety-two miles from their starting point, or elsewhere along the line.

Whatever the case, Henry's train was headed east on track #4 on Saturday, October 3.[9] Retracing his westbound leg, he passed through the Gulf Curve at Little Falls, a dangerous section of track that was the scene of many accidents, both before and since.[10] Fort Plain was next, followed by Yosts, a place where towering cliffs on each side of the tracks marked the great split in the Appalachian Mountains. Then it was on to Fonda, where he likely stopped to pick up or drop off freight cars.

It was three thirty in the afternoon when Henry's locomotive approached Tribes Hill, a place named for the Indian tribes that gathered there a century earlier. The track followed a wide bend that stuck out like a thumb into the Mohawk River. Because the river often flooded at this point, the poles carrying telegraph wires were set tight to the track.

About a mile or two before the train reached a freight depot that served Tribes Hill, Henry moved from the cab of his locomotive to its gangway, the space between the rear of the engine's cab and its tender. Suddenly without warning, he tumbled from the cab, landing hard between the two freight tracks. Either the front brakeman or the fireman dashed into the cab to set the brakes and reverse the engine. The train was brought to a grinding, screeching halt as Henry's crew ran back up the tracks to assist their engineer, who lay unconscious on the track.

Minutes later, the New York Central's *Eastern Express* appeared in the distance on track #2 on its scheduled run from Buffalo to Albany. The pickup's crew flagged it down, and Henry, still unconscious, was placed aboard. The fast express steamed on to its 3:46 PM scheduled stop at Amsterdam where an ambulance was summoned to carry the stricken engineer to the city's St. Mary's Hospital.

News that her husband was injured on the job reached Louisa Horstman, probably early that evening. She had no telephone; that was a luxury only the wealthiest residents could afford. The dreaded news was likely delivered by Henry Bartling, their upstairs boarder, after West Albany received word by telegraph from the Amsterdam station. Henry's brother, Fred, got the news from his wife Rose (nee Gerding) who ran from her house on Ferry Street to the Locomotive Works.

For fifteen years Louisa had kept a lid on her fear that Henry might be seriously hurt on the job. When her husband was on the road she tried not to think of that possibility, assuring herself that *Heinrich* was a good and competent railroad man. Yet the unthinkable had happened.

Louisa set out for the hospital in Amsterdam, probably leaving her four children in the care of her sister, Caroline Lange. There were no automobiles; she may have hired a horse carriage and driver from Hathaway's Livery, or she could have taken a trolley on a new line that connected Schenectady and Amsterdam, a seventeen-mile journey. She didn't know what to expect when she reached the hospital, only that Henry was in an accident. No one in Schenectady had any details about his injuries. News traveled slowly without radio, television, or the Internet.

Like most hospitals of the day, St. Mary's was a dark and dank place. A horse-drawn ambulance had carried Henry there from Tribes Hill less than twenty-four hours earlier. Louisa found her husband lying motionless in a bed too short for his long legs. Even though he had no visible signs of injury, it was obvious he was badly hurt. He was unconscious and his breathing uneven as Louisa spoke to him in their native *Platt Deutsch*.

Doctor Gilbert, a local physician hired by the New York Central to treat injured employees, was at Henry's bedside. The doctor had already concluded that the young engineer, identifiable by his overalls, was suffering from a severe concussion and was not likely to survive. Henry remained unconscious for the next four days, unable to speak or respond, while a disconsolate Louisa remained at his bedside, praying for his recovery. Finally, about ten o'clock in the evening on October 7, her beloved husband breathed his last. It was two weeks before his fortieth birthday.

Louisa returned to Schenectady heartsick and exhausted. Arriving home, she was stunned to find Henry Bartling, the Central engineer who lived upstairs, being treated by a doctor. Bartling had been struck by a "kick" of cars while standing next to his engine. He suffered an apparent concussion but was expected to recover.[11]

Henry's funeral was held on Saturday, October 10 in the Mynderse Street house, the immigrant couple's home for thirteen years. The house overflowed with relatives, friends, and neighbors, many of whom spoke quietly in the language of the Old Country. Members of the BLE's Division No. 172 came to pay last respects to one of their most popular brethren. The grieving widow was presented with a brass bell that likely came from the locomotive her husband was driving at the time of the accident. Later, the Brotherhood's Ladies' Auxiliary provided Louisa with $500, probably the proceeds of an insurance policy Henry had purchased.

Louisa arranged for Henry to be buried next to his daughter Jessie in the cemetery plot that he purchased just five years earlier. His final resting place lies just a short distance from that of his uncle, Friedrich Horstmann, the inspiration for his American Dream. The two enginemen are surrounded by gravestones in a German section of the cemetery that bear the names of fellow Hille emigrants.

Unlike Casey Jones, no ballad or song was composed for Henry Horstman, an engineer who achieved his American Dream only to lose it in one inexplicable, fleeting moment on the rails. Incredibly, there would be no investigation, either by the New York State Railroad Commission or the ICC. It was just another "little accident," easily dismissed by the railroad as the engineer's own fault.

Children of Henry and Louisa Horstman. Photo taken a few months before their father's accident in 1903. From left: Irene, Elmer, Raymond, and Clarence.

Thirteen

"BLAME IT ON THE ENGINEER"

A lurch that flings the rushing train,
A roaring shock that rips and rends,
The groan of death the shriek of pain,
And—Holy Holy Dividends.

The Engineer—poor chap he's killed
That makes the explanation clear
A trusted servant tried and skilled
We'll blame it on the engineer.

(From *The Railroad Trainman*)[1]

Carelessness, the railroads argued, was the root cause of the "little accidents" that took so many lives and generated so many injuries. "It was his own fault," was the usual response when a trainman was killed. That skewed logic enabled the people who were most able to improve safety to blame the hazards on those least able, writes railroad historian Aldrich.[2]

Was Henry's fatal accident his own fault? Except for local newspaper reports, no official record of the accident or his death can be found in city, state, or federal archives; in the Amsterdam hospital where he was taken; or in the records of the now defunct New York Central Railroad. Because his death didn't occur within twenty four hours of the accident, it was not even counted among the nationwide railroad fatalities reported by the ICC. Even so, an ICC report for the last quarter of 1903 titled "A Record Breaking Death List" shows more persons killed than in any other quarter since the agency started counting.[3] Among these fatalities were 210 employees killed by "falling from cars or engines." Incredibly, within a single year at least 457 trainmen were killed and another 4,757 injured due to falling from trains, locomotives, or cars in motion.[4]

There is no evidence that an investigation of Henry's accident was undertaken, either by the ICC or the New York State Board of Railroad Commissioners.[5] While the state's board employed inspectors, they were dispatched to investigate collisions, derailments, and explosions—a one-man accident apparently didn't call for an investigation.

Investigating an accident more than a century after it occurred is a daunting task, one obviously hindered by the lack of living eyewitnesses and public or private records that could help explain the calamity. This leaves newspapers as the only sources of information about what happened on that fateful October day.

Not surprisingly, the newspaper accounts are contradictory. City newspapers in Amsterdam and Schenectady covered the story, but they agree on only a few basic facts: that Henry fell from the engine, suffered a severe head injury, and remained unconscious until his death. They differ markedly as to why he fell and how he received a blow to his head.

The first report of the accident appeared in the *Amsterdam Evening Recorder* on Saturday, October 3: "Horstman was leaning out of the cab window, when his head came in contact with a telephone pole, and he was knocked from his seat." Two days later, the newspaper retreated somewhat: "It has not been fully ascertained whether Horstman fell from the cab of his engine or his head struck some object on the track."

By October 5, two Schenectady newspapers had picked up the story. One, the morning *Gazette,* said the accident happened in "an unaccountable manner" as Horstman "was standing on the gangway of his engine, which was moving rapidly and he either lost his balance and fell to the ground or struck a car on the opposite track." The *Schenectady Daily Union* followed later that day, reporting that the engineer fell from the engine "striking heavily in the 'six foot' space between the two freight tracks."

On October 8, the *Daily Union* reported that Henry's injuries had resulted in his death. "It appears," the newspaper concluded, "that Mr. Horstman lost his balance while standing in the gangway of his engine, the space between the engine cab and the tender, and fell to the ground. The engine was proceeding along at a good rate of speed hauling a heavy freight train … It is believed that his skull was fractured." That same day the *Schenectady Evening Star* ran a front page story about the "singular coincidence" in which two New York Central engineers living in the same house suffered similar accidents.

The author asked three railroad historians to review the newspaper accounts of the accident.[6] One commented that the widely differing reports illustrate how reporters of that era would make up what they couldn't find out. For example, the configuration of the cab on the locomotive (No. 663) would not have allowed the engineer to fall out if he was leaning out the window.

There was consensus among reviewers that Henry was for some reason standing in the gangway and lost his balance, or a handhold gave way and he fell. All agreed that the engineer may have been leaning out of the gangway to get a signal from his brakeman, checking behind for a "hot box," or looking down the tracks for oncoming traffic. Sometimes, they noted, especially on older locomotives, broken steps on the catwalks and missing bolts on grab irons would cause an engineer to fall. Ironically, on the very day of Henry's accident, a New York Central official in West Albany wrote to the ICC complaining that the law requiring grab irons and steps on the pilots of locomotives was dangerous "because they invite employees to place themselves unnecessarily in a dangerous position."[7]

According to New York Central's records, the locomotive Henry was driving (No. 663) was an eighteen-year-old Class C-18, Rogers-built engine that had seen its best days with the New York West Shore and Buffalo Railroad.[8] The engineer's order to return it to the yard for repairs indicate that it was not in good condition. A locomotive of that vintage was known in railroad jargon as a "scrap pile," meaning a worn-out one still in service. More than likely his train was not properly equipped with air brakes. The Central sold the engine fifteen months after Henry's accident.

Working on a freight train was "breathtakingly dangerous," Aldrich writes.[8] Sometimes men were killed or injured by falling off trains from the severe shocks triggered when an unbraked rear section rammed into the forward section. An ICC investigation found that the unusual increase in accidents in 1903 and 1904 was the result of "the deterioration of equipment and the inability of the Commission to secure a full compliance with the law."[10] Its report singled out accidents caused by freight trains buckling when air brakes were applied, noting that "the constant influx of high capacity cars and increase in size and weight of trains calls for an increase in effective braking power."

The railroads' failure to equip freight cars with air brakes or to keep them in repair was a cause of many accidents. The Safety Appliance law required only that a "sufficient" number of a train's cars be equipped with power brakes. In testimony before Congress, a representative of the railroad brotherhoods explained the problem: "If only a portion of the equipped cars are operated, trainmen are exposed to great danger arising from the breakage of an air hose or a coupling between the cars so braked, which causes an instantaneous and extremely powerful application of the power brakes, which causes the front cars in the train to quickly slacken speed and the other cars behind them which are not braked to rush forward against them, thus causing a severe shock, which often wrecks the train and jars the trainmen off and injures them, and in some cases they fall under the wheels and are killed."[11]

Could Henry have been struck by some object, as one news report suggested? It is possible he came into contact with an object, perhaps a stick of lumber protruding from a train on the opposite track, or even another train itself, according to one reviewer. Clearances between the track and adjacent utilities were usually at least five feet. Unless the telegraph poles were "out of gauge," hitting one would be difficult although not impossible. By coincidence, on the same day of Henry's death the *Albany Times Union* reported that an engineer on the *Jersey Central Flyer* was found dead alongside the track. According to the article, he was "knocked from his cab—struck on the head by an automatic signal pole and his neck broken."[12]

Is it possible that Henry, not yet forty years old, suffered a heart attack or stroke and sustained the head injury when he fell to the ground? According to one newspaper, physicians at the hospital "endeavored to find a fracture of the skull, believing that the engineer was suffering from something more serious than concussion, but it was impossible." The final word came from Dr. Gilbert, the railroad's physician, who concluded after a "thorough examination" that Henry had suffered a concussion of the brain.[13]

One reviewer suggests the possibility of a cover-up by the New York Central. He observes that none of the newspaper accounts include any statement from the railroad itself. Nor do they quote, or even mention, the train's fireman, a person who would have known what happened. "While railroad managers were usually anxious to know what caused an accident, they were not anxious to disclose the reasons for it especially if a victim died without regaining consciousness," he says. "Railroads did not earn dividends by paying out compensation. Out-of-gauge items and failed handholds made them liable for compensation. Engineers breaking the rules by hanging out of cabs did not." Further, he notes, "railroad managers were not averse to quietly threaten other workers with discipline in order to silence them."[14]

The cover-up theory is bolstered by the fact that there is no county or city record of an inquest to determine the cause of Henry's death. Nor is there any evidence that a death certificate was filed. Could the railroad's doctor have persuaded the coroner not to conduct an inquest? Without one, there could be no demand by the victim's survivors for compensation. Was the Central's physician more interested in limiting the railroad's expense than in his patient's well-being? Louisa Horstman, it should be noted, received not a cent of compensation from the New York Central.

Even if Louisa had pursued a lawsuit against the railroad for the death of her husband, the railroad enjoyed a host of legal defenses that made it virtually impossible to succeed. Workers were deemed to assume the risks related to their jobs or rising out of the conditions of the workplace. Further, one had to prove negligence by the railroad and that the worker was not at fault—a virtually insurmountable task, especially when the railroad controlled the evidence.

Finally, there remains the likelihood that fatigue played a role in Henry's accident. Unfortunately, the New York Central's employee records have long since disappeared. Without company records there is no way to determine how many hours Henry was on the job prior to the accident, or how many shifts he worked in the days and nights preceding it. But there is ample reason to conclude that the deteriorating locomotive he was assigned to drive—combined with the round-the-clock demands he faced—contributed to the tragic accident.

After a series of deadly railroad accidents in 1997, the *Houston Chronicle* interviewed many trainmen, including a Union Pacific engineer. "Fatigue and long hours is nothing new, it's something that's been going on for a hundred years," he said upon completing a twelve-hour shift after midnight. The newspaper's story was titled "Fatigue puts rail workers on a dangerous track—irregular schedules, antiquated regulations and railroad culture create crews of weary workers running trains."[15] That present-day headline may best describe what happened to engineer Henry Horstman on a fateful October day more than a century ago.

Engineer Horstman was driving a 4-4-0 Class C-18 locomotive
like this one when the accident occurred (photo courtesy
of New York Central System Historical Society)

Postcard dated 1898 shows the close proximity of trains
passing on the New York Central's 4-track line.

Fourteen

ACCOUNTABILITY

*Power corrupts a leader's ability to sense how
the world is experienced by others.*

From a Northwestern University study, 2007[1]

While there can be no certainty about what caused Henry's
accident, or whether or not it was covered up, one thing is
certain. The men who directed and controlled the New York Central
and Hudson River Railroad failed to provide even the semblance of a
safe working place for their employees. "There seems to be a lower value
placed on human life in America," wrote a British engineer who studied
the U.S. rail system in 1906.[2]

Between 1901 and 1904, the New York Central's profits nearly
doubled, rising from $8 million to $15.9 million. At the same time, the
railroad paid less than 1 percent of its annual earnings from passenger
and freight operations for "injuries to persons" (most payouts went to
passengers).[3]

It was well understood at railroads like the New York Central, all
the way through middle managers, that nothing was to change unless
orders came from their CEOs or owners.[4] At the time of Henry's death,
the Central's board of directors included Chauncey Depew (chairman),
William K. Vanderbilt, Frederick W. Vanderbilt, J.P. Morgan, and

William Rockefeller.[5] All directors were vested with the responsibility to oversee the company.

Foremost among them was Senator Depew, who held both the public and private power to rectify the pernicious working conditions that confronted trainmen. Indeed, he served as chairman of the Senate Committee on Revision of the Laws of the United States. He had access to the telling statistics, not only from the ICC's widely publicized accident reports but from his own company's records. Yet he turned a blind eye to the escalating carnage on the rails, choosing instead to work behind the scenes with other railroad senators to block safety measures like the Accident Reporting Act and limits on the number of hours trainmen were required to work.

Senator Depew was respected and even feared by other senators because of his sharp wit and speaking prowess. Yet he never employed those talents on behalf of the men who ran the rails. His betrayal of the company's workers included corruption that deliberately undermined the public's demand for enforceable safety regulations.

The carnage continued unabated after Henry's death in 1903. *Colliers Weekly*, in 1907, observed that train accidents and disasters had become a daily routine, mostly caused by "sleepy train crews or dispatchers who have been working twenty, thirty or forty hours at a stretch." The magazine estimated that over a period of five years "we have allowed the railroads to kill and cripple a population as large as San Francisco."[6]

Headlines like "Railway Massacre" and "Another Railway Horror" shocked the American public.[7] Sites of major collisions or derailments became familiar household words. Travelers were afraid to board trains. Even the founder of the Great Northern Railway, James J. Hill, was moved to exclaim: "Every time I undertake a railroad journey nowadays I wonder whether it is to be my last."[8]

Newspapers demanded action. "Who is the Murderer?" charged the *Washington Post* after it reviewed the ICC's distressing statistics.[9] Casualties from train accidents, it said, "are increasing faster than the mileage, faster than the increase in passenger and freight traffic, faster than the operating expenses or gross income, faster than the money spent on rolling stock or improvements, and faster than the total number of passengers carried."

"Someone is to blame," the *Post* concluded. But the railroad industry had no intention of assuming the blame, or responsibility, for the casualties. They tried to convince a skeptical public that the blame belonged to employees and their unions, arguing that the casualties were the result of a "growing disregard of personal safety manifested by the rank and file."[10] The *Railroad Gazette*, an industry publication, even claimed the railroads' use of safety appliances caused a decline in workers' "cautiousness, efficiency, and discipline."

The railroad brotherhoods responded that the rising casualties were the result of heavy workloads imposed by railroad managers obsessed with increasing tonnage and bottom-line profit. Their men, they said, were under enormous pressure to get work done and were driven by railroad managers to take unnecessary risks. Heavy freights were frequently late, they noted, causing train crews to work longer hours and demoralizing the overworked men. Management was to blame for driving men and equipment to the breaking point.[11]

Taking the railroads on in Congress was a monumental task. Eleven senators, including Depew, all had substantial personal financial interests in railroads.[12] They fought President Roosevelt's proposals to set railroad rates with every means at their disposal. "It was a great misfortune," *The Outlook* observed in 1906, that "such a small group of Senators with interweaving business and political interests ... has corrupted and lowered the tone of our public life."[13]

The railroads fought efforts to impose safety standards on their businesses, contending that Congress shouldn't meddle in matters between railroads and their employees. They opposed tonnage limits, manning requirements and the adoption of automatic stopping devices. They blocked attempts to require railroads to clear their right-of-way for obstructions like telephone poles. They even fought legislation that made it possible for firemen to avoid crawling between a locomotive's driving wheels to empty ash pans.[14]

The most egregious example was their attempt to block President Roosevelt's repeated suggestion (the first in 1903) that Congress place limits on the hours of service that trainmen were required to work.[14] But in 1906 they met their match in "Fighting Bob" La Follette, a freshman senator from Wisconsin. When the railroad senators threatened to filibuster his "Hours of Service Act," La Follette issued a blunt warning:[15]

"If this legislation is withheld from the statute books at this session by such methods, those who have engaged in that business will have to assume the responsibility for whatever casualties may befall the traveling public and the railway employees of this country ..."

Senator La Follette's warning was prophetic. On December 30, 1906, a disastrous train wreck at Terra Cotta, a Maryland town within gunshot of the nation's capital, underscored the urgency of the situation. A Baltimore & Ohio passenger train was rammed from behind by another train. An engineer, dazed with weariness and lack of sleep, had missed a signal and plunged into the passenger train, grinding thirty passengers to their deaths. An investigation quickly revealed that the exhausted engineer had been on duty almost continuously for thirty-three hours and without a full night's rest for fifty-seven hours.[16]

Within days of the Terra Cotta calamity, Senator La Follette disclosed a list of accidents involving train crews who had worked for at least fifteen straight hours without rest. The senator suggested that if his bill to limit trainmen's hours had been in effect it would have averted at least twenty of the twenty-one accidents on the list.[17]

The railroads attacked La Follette's bill, dismissing it as too paternalistic, mischievous, and unnecessary. Unfazed, the senator responded that the number of employees and passengers killed and injured by the railroads over five years had increased by 70 percent—a total of 277,475 people, or, as he put it, "almost as many people as constitute the population of this great national capital."[18] Another senator likened the death toll to the battle of Gettysburg in the Civil War "when two American armies stood up for three days and shot death into each other's bosoms ..."

Sensing the momentum building for La Follette's bill, the railroad senators turned to another favored tactic. They effectively gutted the legislation with amendments, making it look "much like a scarecrow that had been run through a threshing machine," reported the *Washington Times*.[19] But at a critical juncture, La Follette demanded a roll call vote on his original bill. "Brought squarely under the gun," the *Times* observed, "the opposition had neither the courage to defeat La Follette nor the nerve to stand by its worthless substitute." To the amazement of spectators in the Senate gallery, La Follette's bill passed by a 36-32 vote. Senator Depew was among those voting "No."[20]

"The fight was all over when that vote was taken, and the railroad opposition having been beaten on the real test, all ran to the cover of the final roll call and appeared gaily in the affirmative," said the *New York Times*.[21] Senator Depew, it noted, was one who "ran for cover" and voted for the bill, which was passed by an overwhelming vote of 70 to 1 on January 10, 1907. The *Washington Times* called La Follette's victory "complete, sweeping, and unexpected." The landmark bill sailed through the House of Representatives by a 281-to-0 vote and was signed into law by President Roosevelt on March 4, 1907.

For the first time, a federal law directed at the exploitation of railroad workers was on the books. It provided that no railroad could require or permit trainmen to work for more than sixteen hours consecutively, or more than a total of sixteen hours during any twenty-four-hour period. The law also set a minimum of ten consecutive hours of rest after the worker was on duty for sixteen consecutive hours.

Enactment of The Hours of Service Act paved the way for a flood of new laws and regulations to protect trainmen and railroad passengers. One of the most important was the Federal Employers' Liability Act (1908) which abolished a law railroads used to avoid accident liability. The new law raised the cost of casualties to the railroads, forcing them to pay more attention to safety. Still others mandated self-cleaning ash pans (1908); new safety devices on cars and engines like ladders, steps, and hand brakes (1910); more detailed accident reports (1910); and locomotive inspections (1911).[22] Unfortunately, these measures were too late for Henry Horstman and thousands of his fellow trainmen who lost their lives and limbs in the first years of the twentieth century.

As to Senator Depew, an investigation in 1906 revealed that he was secretly receiving an annual payment of $20,000 from the Equitable Life Assurance Society.[23] In the uproar that followed, Republicans in the New York State Assembly drafted a resolution calling on him to resign, citing a "total lack of confidence in the ability of the Senator to properly represent the people in the body to which he was elected ..."[24]

The *New York World* reprinted an earlier interview with Depew titled "Why It Pays to be Honest." *Cosmopolitan* delivered a scathing assessment: "Our history," the magazine declared, "offers no more striking instance of one-man power than the wide paralyzing effect and the vast and sinister economic results of the studied and shallow geniality of this sycophant to a plutocratic family."[25]

Depew continued to serve out his second term in the Senate, gamely pronouncing (on his seventy-sixth birthday) that he intended "to hold on to my job as long as I live." At the same time, he blithely asserted that "no lobby exists at Washington, no interests there seek to influence senators and congressmen."[26] But in 1911 when it came time to run for a third term he quietly withdrew his name from consideration.

Many years later, Depew wrote his autobiography, "My Memories of Eighty Years."[27] One chapter is devoted to his "Fifty-Six Years with the New York Central Railroad Company" (he remained chairman of the railroad until his death in 1928). Depew could just as well have titled his book "Famous People Who Knew Me," as it consists mostly of impressions of famous people he knew—presidents, governors, senators, businessmen, orators, actors, and "men of letters."

Among these prominent figures was P.M. Arthur, chief of the powerful Brotherhood of Locomotive Engineers. Depew had carefully cultivated a friendship with Arthur, a relationship that kept the Central's trains running and enabled the railroad senator to marginalize the union's demands. Yet his book pays no homage to the courageous men who sacrificed their lives and limbs to run the Central's trains. Perhaps he didn't want his trainmen to know what went on in the smoke-filled rooms of the capitals in Albany, New York, and Washington, D.C.

When Depew died on April 5, 1928, the *New York Times* remembered him as "one of the wise men of the Western World" and "an oracle of how to live a useful and contented life."[28]

Afterword:
Renewing the Link

*Too often when writing about immigrants we forget
that there were immigrant losers as well as winners,
and that sometimes winning took generations.*

Roger Daniels, *Coming to America*, 2002[1]

Schenectady County court records show that Henry Horstman died without a will. A local court appointed Louisa to administer his estate.[2] His personal belongings were valued at $1,200, exclusive of the Mynderse Street house. Louisa's brother Charles and her uncle Christian posted bond to cover the estate until it was settled.

Louisa, only thirty-eight years old when her husband died, struggled to raise her four children. Henry's income was sorely missed. The five hundred dollars she received from the Brotherhood of Locomotive Engineers was not adequate to sustain the family. She received nothing from the New York Central, a company that recorded profits of $15.9 million in 1903 and didn't provide benefits for surviving family members.[3]

Social security, a reality in Germany, was yet to be introduced in the United States. With no regular source of income, Louisa had to rely on relatives, probably her brother Charles and her sister, Mary Lange. She may have worked in her uncle Christian's tailor shop to bring in some income. Somehow, she managed to get by for almost three years, but when Charles Derwig, a widowed tailor raising four boys, proposed marriage she had little choice but to accept. After their marriage on September 5, 1906, she moved into Derwig's house on Barrett Street with her four children. It's likely she rented out the Mynderse Street duplex to generate income for the combined families.

Little more than a year after the wedding, Louisa's five-year-old son Elmer contracted diptheria, probably from drinking contaminated water or milk. He was put into quarantine, but his condition worsened, and he died in January 1908. Elmer was the second child that Louisa lost since the new century began. The twentieth century was disastrous for her—in its first eight years she had lost a husband two children.

In December 1909 Henry's younger brother, Fred, who emigrated from Hille in 1883, was thrown from a horse. The forty-four-year-old machinist died soon after from injuries he sustained in the freakish mishap. He was survived by his wife, Rose, and seven children.

The tragic deaths of the two Horstman brothers, Henry and Fred, marked the end of communication between the American Horstman(n) families and their German relatives living on the farm at Hille #29. It would take two World Wars and two generations before contact was reestablished.

When the combined Horstman-Derwig families did not integrate well, Louisa moved her three children back into the Mynderse Street house. Her uncle Christian, who lived with the family in 1910, mesmerized young Raymond with stories about Minden. Despite many hardships, Louisa remained a cheerful woman, even venturing to fly in a Ford tri-motor airplane.

To help support his mother, Raymond became a breadwinner at an early age. He delivered newspapers, worked on farms in Glenville, and took a chauffeur's job driving Buicks. In 1917 he was drafted into the U.S. Army but served only three months as World War I finally came to an end.

Herbert H. and William F. Horstman, sons of Henry's deceased brother, served in the American Expeditionary Force sent to assist the Allies in Europe. Each fought with the U.S. Army's 105th Infantry Regiment (Twenty-seventh Division) in Belgium and France. William, who was twenty-one in 1917, was wounded twice—once in the bloody battle at Argonne Forest. His brother Herb, two years older, fought in the battles of DeMev Ridge, LaBelle River, and the Hindenberg Line. They both survived the conflict and returned to live in Schenectady.

Christian and Heinrich Horstmann, sons of Henry's older brother in Hille, did not fare so well. *Landsturm* recruits in the German Army, they both were wounded on the front lines. In December 1916, Christian sustained a leg injury in France and was sent to Bremen where the old *Auswanderunghaus* was converted into a wartime hospital. Heinrich fought in the terrible battle of Verdun in 1916, also known as the "Mincing Machine of Verdun," one of the bloodiest battles in human history, in which German losses were estimated at 142,000 killed and 187,000 wounded.[4] Heinrich survived the carnage, but he was wounded in August 1918 and taken by the British as a prisoner of war. After the war, Heinrich embarked on a business career while Christian returned to the farm in Hille.

The wartime experiences of German soldiers like Christian and Heinrich Horstmann are portrayed in the great war novel, *All Quiet on the Western Front*. Its German author, Erich Maria Remarque, lived in Osnabruck, a city not far from Hille. He, too, was wounded on the Western Front.

Landsturm recruits Christian (l) and Heinrich Horstmann on
leave from the Front, ca. 1915. Seated are their parents, Marie (nee
Schütte) and Christian H. Horstmann, Henry's brother.

By the end of World War I, Americans with German surnames had
little interest in searching for relatives in Germany. A new generation
wanted to look ahead and forget the horrors of that conflict. With help
from Chester Rankin, a prominent Schenectady businessman, Raymond
Horstman enrolled at Union College in 1918. The immigrant's son
worked summers in the General Electric plant and with a timber crew
at Whiteface Mountain, New York. Graduating in 1923, he and a
partner started the Plywood Real Cover Company, which he ran from
1924 to 1926. In 1927, Raymond helped raise $121,000 to build "Port
Schenectady," the first airport in the nation to be financed wholly by

public subscription. Charles Lindbergh flew his *Spirit of St. Louis* into the new airport that year.

Lindbergh's exploits inspired a new generation of boys to dream about flying airplanes rather than driving locomotives. In 1930, sixteen year-old Marvin "Pewee" Horstman, a descendant of Henry's immigrant uncle Carl Horstmann, earned a license to fly open cockpit biplanes. Forty-two years later, Captain Horstman piloted the aircraft that carried President Nixon on an historic trip into mainland China.[5]

When the Great Depression struck in 1929, Raymond sold Hudson cars and later became a top sales manager for the Easy Washing Machine Company. He remained devoted to his mother throughout her life until she died in January 1937. She was buried next to her true love, Henry Horstman, and their two children, Jessie and Elmer, in the German section of Vale cemetery. On July 10, 1937, Raymond married Jean Douglass, a graduate of nearby Skidmore College. They had two children—the author and Louise Horstman-Code. In 1943, he was elected to the Schenectady County Board of Supervisors where he served on its Post-War Planning Committee.

It wasn't until June 1978 that contact between the American and German Horstmann families was revived. Thanks to Henry's birth certificate and a German telephone directory, I was able to identify a Horstmann family in Westphalia with an address listed as Hille #29. An exchange of letters confirmed this was the place where Henry was born and that Christian Horstmann was a descendant of my grandfather's German family.

My sister and I traveled to Hille, still a small village of well-kept farms and brick houses with steep, sloping, red-tiled roofs. At Hille # 29 we were greeted by Christian who exclaimed in his native *Platt Deutsch* that we were the first Horstmanns to return from America in almost one hundred years. He and his wife, Marie (nee Rüter), lived in the farmhouse along with his daughter Elizabeth Buhrmester and fourteen-year-old Heike, his granddaughter, who spoke excellent English and served as our translator.

Eighty-four-year-old "*Opa*" still limped from the injury he sustained in World War I. The oldest of two sons, he had inherited the Hille farm when his father died in 1926. Proudly he showed us the door beam over the entrance to the main house inscribed with his grandparents' names, Christian Friedrich Horstmann and Caroline Marie (Kasten) Horstmann. He took us to their burial place in the *Friedhof* and the Evangelical Lutheran Church where at least six generations of Horstmanns have worshipped.

Christian's brother Heinrich, a spry eighty-one-year-old, lived in nearby Schoetmar. Greeting us, he asked, "*Welcher Horstmann komst du* (which Horstmann do you come from)?" "*Heinrich, der auswanderer*," we replied.

We learned that after the Great War, Heinrich won several rowing competitions, earning the title "North German Rowing Master." He became a commercial trader and in 1934 started his own company, one that produces eyeglass frames. In 1955, he bought land "in the meadows" near his parent's farm in Hille where he erected a factory. Heinrich married Auguste Schmidt, who died in 1977, the year before our visit. They had three children together—a son also named Heinrich and two daughters, Christiane and Carola. Young Heinrich and stepson Hans Gottfried Schmidt are officers of the company which does business under the name Licefa.

The two elderly Horstmann brothers were children when Henry was killed in the 1903 railroad accident. Their parents learned the sad news from a neighbor in Hille named Gerding who visited Schenectady not long after the accident occurred. Somehow they hadn't been told, or didn't recall, that Henry was survived by a widow and four children. Nor did they know that Henry had married Louisa, a Hille emigrant. Horstmann was a common name in the village, Christian explained, and took us to the house (#232) where Louisa was born.

The timing of our 1978 visit to Germany was providential. In February 1979, Christian Horstmann died at Hille 29. And in December 1980, his brother Heinrich passed away. They were the last Horstmann males to be born at Hille 29.

Horstmann farm, Hille #29, 1978.

Christian and Marie (Rüter) Horstmann with daughter Elizabeth
Buhrmester (left) and granddaughter Heike Buhrmester.

Other descendants of my grandfather's family lived in nearby cities. Heinrich Dreyer's mother, Marie Frederika Horstmann, was born at Hille #29. Heinrich, a veteran of World War II, was severely wounded at the Russian front when a horse wagon rolled over him. He eventually recovered and founded a clothing manufacturing company, Heinrich Dreyer & Company in Obernbeck. His opposition to the Third Reich caused many difficulties for his business. He and his wife Elfriede, had three children—two sons, Heinz-Jurgen (Heiner) and Horst; and a daughter, Gudrun. Both sons were active in the Dreyer family business.

In October 1985 Heinrich Dreyer brought his family to America to meet his Horstman relatives. He and Raymond Horstman, two look-alike cousins, met for the first (and last) time. It was an emotional time for both as they embraced, and Heinrich said to Raymond (in German): "When I look into your eyes, I feel as if I've known you all my life."

Upon his return to Germany, Heinrich wrote to my parents:

Dear Jean!
Dear Raymond!

The Dreyer family has returned to Germany two weeks ago. The value of this journey across the big pond is tremendous. But first of all we had the very great pleasure to become acquainted with the whole Horstman family. All of us, from the youngest to the oldest, are enthusiastic about our American relatives which have their origin in Hille.

Dear cousin Raymond, I would like to thank you for the invitation to the 'family-party,' which has been called forth with great enthusiasm. It is marvelous that you and I, the two seniors of the family, still have the chance to take part in such events.

I am of the opinion that you in America and we here in Germany, in spite of the fact that we have grown up under such different circumstances, dispose about a very similar view about life, the kind of life above all—about the family.

And this attitude will unite us even over the great distance. All of us, especially myself, have become fond of you! And we wish that this connection will also exist between the next generation.

I wish that you, Jean, and you, Raymond, will be in the best of health further on and that we will have the great pleasure to see you again.

I, your cousin Heinrich, remain with best wishes.

My father later described this one-time meeting with his German cousin as one of the happiest events of his life. He wrote this to Louise and me:

I have thought much about what you have done and how much it means to me to finally be tied in with such a good background. When you think that here in Schenectady was a mother (your grandmother) with four fatherless children stranded in the New World with few ties to turn to, even I can't tell you how she got us through and how you and I are where we are. One thing I always felt was that with the little I knew, my inheritance of body was good and a Christian background was around me. What you have done will always be a major event in my life and I am sure a lasting one in Louise's and your life, and your family's life.

Cousins Raymond Horstman (left) and Heinrich Dreyer meet for first time as Louise Horstman (left) and Tilly Brueggenthies look on (Fairfax, Virginia, October 1985).

133

Horstman-Dreyer family reunion in America
(Fairfax, Virginia, October 1985).

Raymond Horstman and Heinrich Dreyer are now gone. But as they hoped, the once-lost family connection is thriving thanks to e-mail and to trans-Atlantic flights that take a mere eight hours in contrast to the ten-day seagoing voyage that brought seventeen-year-old Heinrich Horstmann to America's shores.

In May 2008 my wife and I attended the wedding of Hendrik Dreyer (son of Horst and Kate Dreyer) in Osnabruck, Germany. It was a joyful event that brought us together with many Horstmann and Dreyer descendants of the Hille Horstmann family. Engineer Henry Horstman's spirit was surely present during the church ceremony.

We also visited the Hille #29 farm, now redesignated as *Am Teich 36*. It is occupied by Heike Vorrath, the granddaughter of Christian Horstmann; her husband Horst, and their four boys—Thilo, Ivo, Laszlo, and Malo. Like the generations before them, the family worships in the ancient Hille church not far from a cemetery where many Horstmanns rest.

Later, we followed the Weser River north to Bremerhaven where a newly constructed museum, *Deutsches Auswanderer Haus*, relates the story of the 4.1 million Germans who emigrated to the New World from that seaport between 1830 and 1974.[6] Standing on the wharf where my grandfather embarked in 1881, I imagined him on the overcrowded deck of the *S.S. Donau* as it headed out into the foreboding North Sea, his destiny uncertain. Although Henry ultimately lost his life, he achieved his American Dream in more ways than he could imagine. His legacy now extends to four generations, the "winners" of his fateful decision to come to America.

ACKNOWLEDGMENTS

The scarcity of primary source material about my grandfather was a motivating factor in my effort to unearth and chronicle his life-story. So, too, was historian David McCullough's admonition to value "what our own parents and grandparents did for us, or we're not going to take it very seriously, and it can slip away."[1]

I am especially indebted to relatives in America and Germany who enthusiastically shared their knowledge about my grandfather and the Horstmann family in Hille. A generation of them has now passed away but their inspiration is reflected in this book. They include Raymond Horstman (my father), Lewis Horstman, Christian and Heinrich Horstmann, Elizabeth Buhrmester, and Heinrich Dreyer.

I interviewed Lewis Horstman in Glenville, New York, shortly before has passed away in December 2006. A second generation descendant of Henry's immigrant uncle Carl (Charles) Horstmann, Lew related stories about my grandfather that he learned from his parents.

Many thanks also to a younger generation of Horstmann descendants in Germany whose assistance was indispensable: Heike Vorrath, Heinz-Jurgen (Heiner) Dreyer, Horst Dreyer, and Heinrich Horstmann. A special thanks to cousin Heiner Dreyer who graciously served as a family liaison while assisting the author with research and translation.

Vital records of the Evangelical Lutheran Church in Hille, made accessible by the Church of Jesus Christ of Latter-Day Saints in Salt Lake City, enabled me to sort out generations of family members who not only had the same surname but often shared identical first names.

Wolfgang Riechmann's *Vivat Amerika* provides a detailed account of emigration from the Minden District of Westphalia and includes the names of twelve thousand emigrants who departed from that region between 1890 and 1933. Passenger ship manifests preserved by the U.S. National Archives in Washington, D.C., are the primary source of information for finding ancestors who arrived in America on immigrant ships.

For further background on German emigration, I consulted *The Uprooted*, Oscar Handlin's Pulitzer Prize–winning epic; Mack Walker's *Germany and the Emigration, 1816–1885;* and letters published in *News from the Land of Freedom: German Immigrants Write Home* (edited by William D. Kamphoefner and others).

For descriptions of life in Schenectady at the turn of the century, I relied on books and photographs produced by Larry Hart, the city's late historian. His two-volume series titled *Tales of Old Schenectady*, together with *Schenectady's Golden Era, 1880–1930* and *Schenectady: A Pictorial History*, provide a fascinating look at this once-great manufacturing city. Thomas A. Reimer's research on the German-American communities in Schenectady and Albany was especially insightful. The Schenectady County Historical Society is the repository of a wealth of historical material for researchers that includes old city directories, newspaper articles, and photographs.

Thanks also to Dick Barrett, a director of the New York Central System Historical Society (NYCSHS), who shared his encyclopedic knowledge of the New York Central Railroad and offered insight as to the possible causes of my grandfather's accident. Mark Aldrich's latest book, *Death Rode the Rails: American Railroad Accidents and Safety, 1828–1965,* is the preeminent source of information on the subject of railroad safety. A telephone interview with Professor Aldrich placed my grandfather's accident in the context of those hazardous times.

When it comes to writing about the lives of steam age trainmen, one must always turn to John H. White, Jr., a former Curator of Transportation at the Smithsonian Institution's National Museum of American History. He is a prolific author whose lively articles in *Railroad History*, a publication which he once edited, bring the era of steam back to life again.

In Washington, D.C., I found annual reports of the now-defunct Interstate Commerce Commission in the library of the U.S. Department of Transportation. The U.S. Library of Congress furnished a wide variety of turn-of-the-century newspapers, railroad publications, photographs, and back editions of the *Congressional Record*. The New York State Library in Albany, New York, provided annual reports of the New York Central and Hudson River Railroad.

Two pertinent structures, an old one in the New World and a new one in the Old World, were the "book ends" for my research. In Manhattan, I toured what remains of Castle Garden, the nation's first immigrant landing depot, where my grandparents first set foot on American soil. And in Bremerhaven, at a newly constructed German Emigration Center, I boarded a replica of an emigrant ship that simulated their journeys across the Atlantic.

Last but not least, I thank my wife, Sondra Rose Horstman, and my sister, Louise Horstman Code, for their encouragement and willingness to travel wherever the story led me.

A final note. This book is not a substitute for a comprehensive genealogy of the Horstman(n) family. While I have made every effort to verify names and dates, the responsibility for any errors that may be unearthed by future family researchers is solely mine.

Douglass C. Horstman
September 2009

Notes

Preface

1. U.S. military casualties in the Iraq War include 4,262 killed and 31,156 injured (March 2003-March 2009). See Iraq Coalition Casualty Count (www.icasualties.org).
2. Quote from Allen, *Liberty: The Statue and the American Dream*, p. 295.
3. Beebe, *High Iron*, p. 3.

Prologue: A Dangerous Occupation

1. See Harlow, *A Treasury of Railroad Folklore*, pp. 449–450.
2. Worker casualty figures are for the year ending June 30, 1904. See *Eighteenth Annual Report of the U.S. Interstate Commerce Commission*, December 19, 1904, p. 97.
3. *Das Buch zum Deutschen Auswandererhaus/The Book to the German Immigration Center*, p. 20.
4. Daniels, *Coming to America*, p. 28.

One. Homeland without Hope

1. Bismarck's quote in E.J. Feuchtwanger, *Prussia, Myth and Reality*, p. 183.
2. See birth certificate in Appendix.
3. H.J. Dreyer interview with Herrn von Behren, Hartum, May 2005.
4. See "*Hiller Hofe*" (www.klemme.org/hausnummern.html).
5. H. J. Dreyer interview with Herrn von Behren.
6. Handlin, *The Uprooted* (1st ed.), pp. 9–10.
7. Handlin, *A Pictorial History of Immigration*, p.131.
8. Handlin, *The Uprooted* (1st ed.), p.108.

9. The *Erweckungsbewegung*, or "awakening" movement was founded by Pastor Volkening of Hille.
10. Church records are on microfilm at the Church of Jesus Christ of Latter-Day Saints in Salt Lake City, Utah.
11. Hille tax records indicate the previous owner was a person named Toedel or Toetels.
12. Details from *"School Situation in Hille, 1800–1900,"* a report by H.J. Dreyer, July 12, 2004.
13. See Craig, *Germany: 1866–1945*, pp.186–192.
14. Translation: "Christian Friedrich Horstmann and Caroline Marie Horstmann, born Kasten, built this house on June 10, 1874."
15. See Info 21, Mindener Museum, 1996.
16. Falk, *History of Germany*, p. 216.
17. Seaton, *The Army of the German Empire, 1870–1888*, p. 25.
18. For details of the depression see Craig, p. 98.

Two. *Auf Wiedersehen*

1. Handlin (2nd. ed.), p. 30.
2. Eric Vanhaute, et. al., *The European Subsistence Crisis of 1845–1850*, IEHC Session 123, Helsinki, 2006.
3. French language entries in the Hille church-books start in 1807 and last for the better part of seven years.
4. Wilhelm H. Horstmann of Cassel later emigrated to the United States and became the founder of a business in Philadelphia (Wm. H. Horstmann Company) that produced military equipment during the U.S. Civil War. See Bazelon, *Horstmanns: The Enterprise of Military Equipage*, p. 2.
5. Mack Walker, *Germany and the Emigration, 1816–1885*, pp. 4–8.
6. See *The Immigration Diary of Michael Friedrich Radke, 1848*, a Radke family history published in 1982.
7. See North German Lloyd advertisement in Wall, *Ocean Liners*, p. 57. Also *Harper's Weekly*, May 22, 1882, p. 330.
8. Walker, p. 182.

9. Kamphoefner, *News from the Land of Freedom: German Immigrants Write Home,* pp. 37–8. Also see further discussion in Riechmann, *Vivat Amerika: Auswanderung aus dem Kreis Minden, 1816–1933.*

10. See Reichmann, pp. 217, 441.

11. Wall, *Ocean Liners,* p. 59.

12. See Reichmann, p. 622.

13. A trading city formed as part of a medieval trade guild.

14. Literally "trappers of green horns." See Dorothy and Thomas Hoobler, *The German American Family Album,* p. 25.

15. Ibid., p. 25.

16. See Mary Cable, "Damned Plague Ships and Swimming Coffins," *American Heritage,* August 1960, p. 96. Also see Walker, p. 89.

17. *Kleindeutschland* was a densely populated German neighborhood around Tompkins Square Park in the Lower East Side of New York.

18. Entry appears on passenger manifest of *S.S. Donau,* April 22, 1881 (line 497) in *Passenger Lists of Vessels Arriving at New York, 1820–1897* (microfilm no. M237, Roll 435), U.S. National Archives and Records Administration, Washington, D.C.

Three. Atlantic Crossing

1. See www.theshipslist.com/ships/descriptions.

2. Cable, p. 97.

3. Ibid.

4. See Charles Dougherty, "The Transatlantic Steamship Captains," *Harpers New Monthly Magazine,* August 1886, pp. 387-9.

5. Jones, Destination America, p. 44.

6. Ibid., p. 40.

7. See theshipslist.com.

8. This account from Kamphoefner, et al., *News from the Land*

of Freedom: German Immigrants Write Home, pp.409–411.

9. See "Shipwrecked and Storm-Beaten," *New York Times*, April 23, 1881.

10. This account from "A Sea Captain's Day's Work," *World's Work Magazine*, April 1901.

11. "Marine Intelligence," *New York Times*, April 23, 1881.

12. Passenger totals from recap on last page of *Donau's* manifest.

13. See "The Flow of Immigration," *New York Times*, April 22, 1881.

14. Adams, *The German-Americans: An Ethnic Experience* (American Edition), p. 4.

15. Melville quoted in Allen, *Liberty: The Statue and the American Dream*, p. 83.

Four. A Place Called Hell

1. See "Before Ellis Island: Castle Garden," *American History Illustrated*, September/October, 1990, pp. 38–9.

2. From "A Scene in Castle Garden," *Harper's Weekly*, February 2, 1889, pp. 86–87.

3. See Jones, *Destination America*, pp. 52–4.

4. Ibid., p. 34.

5. Quote from "Before Ellis Island: Castle Garden," *American History Illustrated*, September/October, 1990, pp. 38–39.

6. Allen, p. 81.

7. Burrows and Wallace, *Gotham: A History of New York City to 1898*, p. 948.

8. Ibid., p. 1054.

9. Ibid., pp. 1111–12.

10. Ibid., p. 1064.

11. Described in Finney, *Time and Again*, p. 399.

12. For complete description of Vanderbilt's mansion, see Hoyt, *The Vanderbilts and Their Fortunes*, pp. 239–241.

13. See Klein, *The History of the New York Central System*, p. 45.

Five. Transformation

1. Reimer, "Distant Thunder: The German American Clergy of Schenectady, New York, and the European War, 1914–1917," *New York History Quarterly Journal,* July 1992 (No. 3), p. 293.
2. See *Passenger Lists of Vessels arriving at New York, 1820–1897*, Microfilm Roll No. 441, U.S. National Archives and Records Administration, Washington, D.C.
3. See *Images of America: Glenville*, Schenectady County Historical Society, 2005.
4. Descriptions of life in the city from Hart, *Schenectady's Golden Era (1880–1930).*
5. See Rev. H.A.Maser, "German Methodist Church History," *Schenectady Union Star*, June 26, 1924.
6. An undated church obituary states that "he came to Schenectady in 1881, where in 1887 under the leadership of Rev. F.H. Rey, he joined our community, to which he remained loyal until his death."
7. See John H.White, Jr., "Oh, To Be a Locomotive Engineer," *Railroad History,* No. 190, Spring–Summer 2004, p. 67.
8. Locomotive building is described in *Railways & Trains*, pp. 20–1.
9. John H. White, Jr., *The American Railroad Freight Car*, p. 152.
10. Botkin and Harlow, *A Treasury of Railroad Folklore*, p. 497.
11. Find a complete account in "The Latest Railroad Disaster," *Harper's Weekly*, January 21, 1882.
12. "New York Central System," *Encyclopedia of North American Railroads*, 2007 ed., p. 746.
13. Hoyt, *The Vanderbilts and Their Fortunes*, p. 175.
14. Vanderbilt, *Fortune's Children*, p. 39.
15. Renehan, *Commodore: The Life of Cornelius Vanderbilt,* p. 325.
16. Vanderbilt, pp. 53–4.
17. See account in Klein, *The History of the New York Central*

System, pp. 55 and 57.

18. Vanderbilt, p. 70.
19. Burrows & Wallace, *Gotham*, p. 1028.
20. See Vanderbilt, p.79; Klein, p. 52; and Harlow, pp. 329–30.
21. Vanderbilt, p. 71.
22. Harlow, pp. 332–3.
23. Ibid., p. 81; Hoyt, p. 261.
24. Hoyt, p. 263.
25. See various accounts in Vanderbilt, pp. 77, 141; Klein, pp. 47–8; and Hoyt, pp. 263–4.
26. Hoyt, p. 274.
27. See *Encyclopedia of North American Railroads*, 2007 ed., p. 10.
28. Klein, p. 54.
29. Harlow, *The Road of the Century*, p. 288.
30. White, Jr., *The American Railroad Freight Car*, p. 77.
31. Stromquist, *A Generation of Boomers*, pp. 106–7.
32. Ibid., p. 108.
33. Richardson, *The Locomotive Engineer 1863–1963*, p. 196.
34. See Stromquist's book on this subject.
35. See White, Jr., "Once It Was Every Boy's Ambition," *Railroad History*, No. 189, Fall–Winter 2003, p. 14.
36. An account of this accident appears in Hubbard's *Railroad Avenue*, pp. 93–4.
37. The hiring process is described in Licht, *Working for the Railroad*, pp. 49–56.
38. This was a title created by George H. Daniels, the New York Central's passenger agent, in 1890. See Harlow, p. 40.

Six. Fireboy on the New York Central

1. See various accounts in *The American Railway*, pp. 391, 411.
2. Sinclair, *Locomotive Engine Running and Management*, seventeenth ed., 1890.
3. See Hubbard's vocabulary of railroad lingo in *Railroad Avenue*, p. 349.

4. A typical manual was the *Rules of the Operating Department* issued by the New York Central and Hudson River Railroad Company, January 19, 1908.
5. Stromquist, *A Generation of Boomers,* p. 116.
6. John H. White, Jr., *The American Railroad Freight Car,* p. 76.
7. Recounted in Aldrich, *Safety First,* p. 184.
8. John H. White, Jr., "Once it Was Every Boy's Ambition" in *Railroad History,* Fall–Winter 2003, p. 16.
9. Aldrich, *Death Rode the Rails,* p. 104.
10. Stromquist, p. 112.
11. Related by Hubbard, p. 284.
12. Stromquist, p. 246.
13. The ICC's 1890 statistics cited in Aldrich, *Death Rode the Rails,* p. 103.
14. Ibid.
15. First annual message to Congress, December 3, 1889 (see Presidential Documents Archive at the American Presidency Project, www.americanpresidency.org).
16. Aldrich, *Safety First,* p. 5.
17. Aldrich, *Death Rode the Rails,* p. 95.
18. *New York Central Highlights,* Quarter 1, 2007, pp.17, 19. See also *Railroad History,* spring–summer 2007, p. 25.
19. For a full account of Engine 999's controversial run, see Thomas Meehan, *Fact or Fable? Railroad History,* spring–summer 2007, p. 47.
20. See Charles W. McDonald, *The Federal Railroad Safety Program,* August 1993, p. 6.
21. For more about Coffin see White, Jr., *The American Railroad Freight Car,* pp. 517–18; and Aldrich, *Safety First,* p. 33.
22. Kurt Wetzel, "Railroad Management's Response to Operating Employees Accidents, 1890–1913," *Labor History,* No.3, summer 1980.
23. Richard Reinhardt, *Workin' on the Railroad,* p. 19.

Seven. Life and Death in Electric City

1. For an account of the growth of Edison Machine Works and other companies in Schenectady see Hart, *Schenectady's Golden Era, 1880–1930,* preface and pp.1–7.
2. See Appendix.
3. He died of throat cancer. See Sturmer, *The German Century,* p.13.
4. Robert D. Parmet, "The Presidential Fever of Chauncey Depew," *Quarterly Journal of New York Historical Society,* July 1970 (No. 54), p. 274.
5. See Depew's speech to a reunion of Union Army veterans, quoted in Parmet, p. 274.
6. The railroad's average number of employees for 1888, according to Fletcher W. Hewes in *The American Railway,* p. 446.
7. Senator Teller quoted in Parmet, p. 287.
8. Ibid., p.279.
9. Ibid.
10. See *Schenectady Union-Star,* June 26, 1948.
11. According to records of Calvary Methodist Church, a successor of the German Methodist Church in Schenectady.
12. Henry's mortgage was filed with the Schenectady County clerk's office on August 8, 1890.
13. Robert E. Weir, "Dress Rehearsal for Pullman: The Knights of Labor and the 1890 New York Central Strike," an essay in *The Pullman Strike and the Crisis of the 1890s,* pp. 21–42.
14. See Reimer, *German-American Ethnicity in Albany, N.Y. 1888–1908,* p. 34.
15. Weir, p. 27.
16. See *New York Times,* August 22, 1890.
17. Reported in the *New York Times,* August 13, 1890.
18. Weir, p. 27.
19. Ibid., pp. 32–5.
20. Don Rittner, "Remains of Schenectady's First Municipal Water Supply Found," *Schenectady County Historical Society*

Newsletter, September-October 2006.

21. From *A History of the Schenectady Turn Verein* by Lisa Schlensker, July 6, 2004.
22. Adams, *The German- Americans: An Ethnic Experience*, p. 27.
23. See Dr. Robert Pascucci, "Electric City Immigrants: Italians and Poles of Schenectady, NY, 1880–1930," Schenectady Digital History Archive, Schenectady County Public Library.
24. Reimer, "Distant Thunder: The German-American Clergy of Schenectady, N.Y. and the European War, 1914-1917," *New York History Quarterly Journal*, July 1992 (no.3), p. 293.
25. Their songs appear in Sullivan's *Our Times: Pre-War America*, pp. 388-9.
26. Reimer, *German-American Ethnicity in Albany, N.Y. 1888-1908*, p. 3.
27. Ibid., p. 45.

Eight. An Extravagant Depression

1. Painter, *Standing at Armageddon*, p. 116.
2. Morris, *The Tycoons*, p. 236.
3. Burrows & Wallace, *Gotham*, p. 1168.
4. See R. Schneirov, S. Stromquist, and N. Salvatore, *The Pullman Strike and the Crisis of the 1890s.*
5. H.W. Brands, *The Reckless Decade*, pp.74–9.
6. Quote from Painter, p. 134.
7. Brands, p. 96.
8. See Hoyt, *The Vanderbilts and their Fortunes*, and Vanderbilt, *Fortune's Children.*
9. Ibid., p. 314.
10. Hart, *Schenectady's Golden Era, 1880–1930*, p. 15.
11. Ibid.
12. Reimer, *Ethnicity in Albany, N.Y. 1888-1908*, pp. 45-46.
13. 1,588 firemen were paid $1,028,663 in the 1893–94 fiscal

year, according to the railroad's 1894 annual report.

14. From records of *Evangelische Kirche* in Hille.

Nine. At the Throttle

1. See White, "Oh, To Be a Locomotive Engineer," *Railroad History*, Spring–Summer 2004, pp. 61–2.
2. Cleveland Moffit, "At the Throttle," *McClure's Magazine*, September 1893, p. 360.
3. *Encyclopedia of North American Railroads*, p. 1063.
4. Orr, *Set Up Running*, p. 2.
5. Ibid., p. 2 and *Encyclopedia of North American Railroads*, p. 1063.
6. Hans W. Gatzke, *Germany and the United States: A Special Relationship?*, p. 44.
7. See White, "Oh, To Be a Locomotive Engineer," *Railroad History*, No. 190, p. 59 (wages are for the year 1900).
8. Vale Cemetery records in Schenectady, N.Y. indicate he purchased it on April 23, 1898.
9. Stromquist, p. 107.
10. *Encyclopedia of North American Railroads*, p. 10.
11. Ibid., p. 95.
12. Aldrich, *Safety First*, p. 169.
13. *Encyclopedia of North American Railroads*, p. 945. Also see Ely, *Railroads & American Law*, p. 213–19, and Aldrich, *Death Rode the Rails*, pp.159–161.

Ten. The Railroad Senator

1. Biography of Chauncey Depew, *Encyclopedia of American Business History and Biography*, p. 93.
2. Depew, *Life and Later Speeches of Chauncey Depew*, p. xvi.
3. Huntington quote from J. Bradford DeLong, *Robber Barons*, University of California at Berkeley, January 1, 1998.
4. See Klein, *New York Central System*, pp. 44–5.

5. Phillips, "*Treason of the Senate,*" *Cosmopolitan Magazine* (Academic Reprints) pp. 15–6.

6. Ibid.

7. Biography of Chauncey Depew, *Encyclopedia of American Business History and Biography*, p. 92.

8. Sullivan, *Our Times: Pre-War America,* p. 208 (fn).

9. Ibid., p. 205.

10. Ibid., p. 209.

11. A Surprising Revelation," Olean, New York *Weekly Democrat,* October 24, 1889.

12. Sullivan, p. 208 (fn).

13. Account reported in Hagerstown, Maryland *Herald & Torch Light*, November 27, 1890.

14. Sullivan, p. 207.

15. Depew, *My Memories of Eighty Years*, pp. 244–5.

16. Robert D. Parmet, "The Presidential Fever of Chauncey Depew," *Quarterly Journal of the New York Historical Society*, July 1970, p. 271 (fn).

17. See Senator-elect Depew's speech as reported in the *New York Times*, February 25, 1899.

18. "State Railroad Commission Report," *The New York Times*, January 13, 1902.

19. See biography of J.P. Morgan in *Encyclopedia of North American Railroads*, p. 719.

20. Hoyt, p. 335.

21. See Reimer, *German-American Ethnicity in Albany, N.Y.1888-1908*, p. 34.

Eleven. In the Shadow of Casey Jones

1. See 1900 annual report of the New York Central and Hudson River Railroad.

2. *12th Census of the United States, Special Report— Occupations,* 1900.

3. McQueen's story appeared in the February 1900 *Saturday Evening Post.*

4. Account of accident from home page of Brotherhood of Locomotive Engineers (www.ble.org).

5. From *Locomotive Engineers Journal*, Winter 1999, Volume 106, No.4.

6. White, "Oh, To Be a Locomotive Engineer," *Railroad History*, Spring–Summer 2004, p. 61.

7. Senator Wolcott's comments from the *Congressional Record*, March 2, 1901.

8. See *Eighteenth Annual Report of the Interstate Commerce Commission*, December 19, 1904.

9. Aldrich, *Death Rode the Rails*, p. 97.

10. Partial listing from Vol. XX, No. 1, January 1903.

11. See *Eighteenth Annual Report of the Interstate Commerce Commission*, p.114.

12. Reinhardt, *Workin' on the Railroad*, p. 20.

13. Ibid.

14. See accounts in Zimmerman, *Twentieth Century Limited*, pp. 33–5 and Harlow, *Road of the Century*, p. 413.

15. See *The Water Level Route*, National Railway Historical Society (Rochester Chapter), p. 27.

Twelve. A Dream Derailed

1. Quotation from Aldrich, *Death Rode the Rails*, p. 4.

2. "City's Rate of Growth Hit Peak in 1900-10," *Schenectady Union-Star*, June 26, 1948.

3. See Hart, *Schenectady: A Pictorial History*, p. 122.

4. The average daily compensation for enginemen in 1903 was $4.01, according to U.S. Commerce Department, *Statistics of Railways in the United States*, p. 43.

5. Accident reports from the New York State Board of Railroad Commissioners, *Twenty-First Annual Report*, Albany, New York, January 11, 1904.

6. "P.M. Arthur Passes; A New Era Begins," *BLE History*, www.ble.org.

7. Botkin and Harlow, *A Treasury of Railroad Folklore*, p. 449.

8. "Engineer Horstman Badly Hurt," *Amsterdam Evening Recorder*, October 5, 1903.
9. The account of his run is based upon local newspaper reports and the *Official Guide of the Railways*, October 1903.
10. See Taylor and Parker, *Night of Disaster—the New York Central Gulf Curve Wreck*.
11. "Both Lived in Same House," *Schenectady Gazette*, Friday, October 9, 1903.

Thirteen. "Blame it on the Engineer"

1. Aldrich, *Safety First*, p. 191.
2. Aldrich, *Death Rode the Rails*, p. 97.
3. Interstate Commerce Commission, *Bulletin #10*, April 29, 1904.
4. *Nineteenth Annual Report of the Interstate Commerce Commission,* December 14, 1905, p. 87.
5. No report appears in the 1903 annual report of the Board of Railroad Commissioners of the State of New York.
6. Reviewers were Mark Aldrich, author of *Death Rode the Rails*; Richard Barrett, a director of the New York Central System Historical Society; and Ray State, a researcher of railroad accidents and wrecks.
7. Letter from C.H. Quereau, Superintendent of Shops, to ICC, dated October 3, 1903.
8. See William D. Edson and H.L. Vail, Jr., *Steam Locomotives of the New York Central Lines*, Volume 1, p.82.
9. Aldrich, *Death Rode the Rails*, p. 105.
10. *Nineteenth Annual Report of the Interstate Commerce Commission*, December 14, 1905, pp. 171–2.
11. Statement of H.R. Fuller to the House Committee on Interstate and Foreign Commerce Committee, February 25, 1902.
12. "Train Ran Miles without Engineer," *Albany Times Union*, October 8, 1903.

13. *Schenectady Gazette,* October 5, 1903, p. 1.
14. Response from Mr. Ray State, dated August 16, 2006.
15. *Houston Chronicle*, August 9, 2005.

Fourteen. Accountability

1. See *U.S. News and World Report*, January 29, 2007.
2. Aldrich, *Safety First*, p. 24.
3. Statistics from the Central's annual reports to shareholders for the years ending in June 1901, 1902, 1903, and 1904.
4. Telephone interview with Mark Aldrich, October 12, 2006.
5. New York Central and Hudson River Railroad, *Annual Report to Shareholders, 1903*.
6. "Our Overworked Railroads," *Colliers Weekly*, January 19, 1907.
7. Aldrich, *Death Rode the Rails*, p. 183.
8. Quoted in "The Death Roll of Industry," *Charities and the Commons*, February 2, 1907.
9. *Washington Post*, December 27, 1904.
10. Wetzel, "Railroad Management's Response to Operating Employees Accidents, 1890–1913," *Labor History*, p. 361.
11. Ibid., pp. 358-9.
12. Sullivan, p. 221.
13. Ibid., p. 221.
14. Wetzel, p. 358.
15. *Congressional Record*, June 29, 1906, p. 9684.
16. "Engineer in Wreck was on Duty 33 Hours," *New York Times*, January 5, 1907.
17. *Congressional Record-Senate*, January 9, 1907, p. 813.
18. Ibid., p. 886.
19. "La Follette Wins After Hard Fight," *Washington Times*, January 11, 1907.
20. *Congressional Record-Senate*, January 9, 1907, p. 891.
21. "Law Limiting Hours of Trainmen Passed," *New York Times*, January 11, 1907.
22. See *Encyclopedia of North American Railroads*, 2007 ed., p.

946.
23. Sullivan, pp. 65-6.
24. "Depew's Soiled Toga Demanded," *New York Sun*, January 4, 1906.
25. See "Treason of the Senate," *Cosmopolitan Magazine*, March 1906.
26. "Depew Determines to Hold His Job," *New York Times*, April 24, 1910.
27. Depew, *My Memories of Eighty Years*, 1921.
28. Quote appears in "Famous New Yorkers," *Syracuse Post-Standard*, November 9, 2005.

Afterword

1. Quotation is from Daniels, *Coming to America*, 2002 (second edition), p. 28.
2. Petition filed by Louisa Horstman with Surrogate's Court of Schenectady County on November 21, 1903.
3. See New York Central and Hudson River Railroad, *Annual Report to Shareholders, 1903*.
4. See "Battle of Verdun" in Wikipedia.
5. "JFK G.M.'s-Flying Hold Reunion," *TWA Skyliner*, November 12, 1979. (Captain Charles Marvin Horstman, a TWA pilot, was born in Glenville, N.Y. on August 1, 1914. He died in 2005 at age 91.)
6. See *Das Buch zum Deutschen Auswandererhaus*, p. 26.

Acknowledgments

1. McCullough's quote is from his speech "Knowing History and Knowing Who We Are," delivered February 15, 2005, at the Hillsdale College National Leadership seminar.

APPENDIX

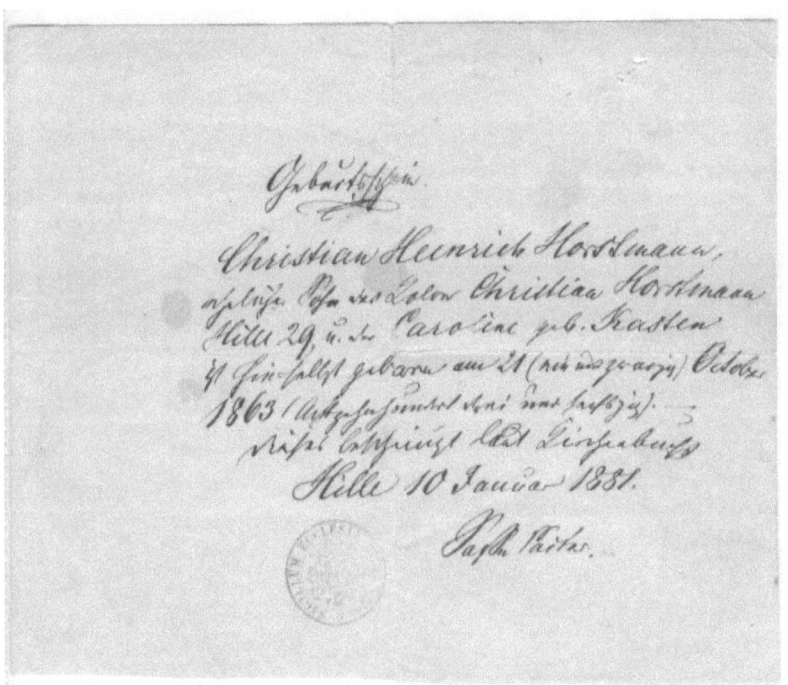

Birth Certificate of Henry (Heinrich) Horstmann

In the matter of the application of

Henry Horstmann }

an alien, for Naturalization.

Fred. Horstmann and *John Slater* being duly sworn, do severally, and each for himself say, that he has known *Henry Horstmann* the present applicant for Naturalization for upwards of five years immediately preceding this application ; during which said five years the said *Henry Horstmann* has continued to reside in the United States, and during, at least one year, has resided in the State of NEW YORK. AND FURTHER, that the said *Henry Horstmann* has, as these deponents believe, during the whole of the five years, behaved as a man of good moral character, attached to the Principles of the Constitution of the United States, and well disposed to the happiness and good order of the same. AND FURTHER, each of these deponents does for himself say that he is a citizen of the United States.

Subscribed and Sworn in open Court, this

30th day of *July* 188*8*. } *Fred Horstmann*

E. L. Milmine Deputy. Clerk. *John Slater*

Henry Horstmann of the *City of Schenectady N.Y.* do swear that I will support the Constitution of the United States, and that I do absolutely and entirely renounce and adjure all allegiance and fidelity to every Foreign Prince, Potentate, State or Sovereignty whatever, and particularly to *William II King of Prussia Emperor of united Germany* or other Sovereignty or Government of those Countries or Territories or either of them.

Sworn in open Court, the

30th day of *July* 188*8*. } *Henry Horstmann*

E. L. Milmine Deputy Clerk.

Naturalization Application of Henry Horstmann

DISTRICT OF NEW-YORK — PORT OF NEW-YORK.

Passenger Manifest of S.S. Donau (partial)

Heinrich Christian Horstmann Full birth name of husband Christian Friedrich Horstmann His father Marie Caroline Kasten His mother with maiden name	Birth date: 21 October 1863 Birth place: #29 Hille, Kreis Minden, Prussia Death date: 7 October, 1903 Death place: Schenectady, New York Burial place Vale Cemetery, Schenectady, New York	
Louisa Marie Horstmann Full maiden name of wife Christian Heinrich Horstmann Her father Christine Marie Elizabeth Buttmann Her mother with maiden name	Birth date: 7 March, 1865 Birth place: # 232 Hille, Kreis Minden, Prussia Death date: 27 January, 1937 Death place: Schenectady, New York Burial place: Vale Cemetery, Schenectady, New York	

Comments	Marriage date, place, etc.
Henry and Louisa dropped the second 'n' from their married name sometime after he became a U.S. citizen in 1888. Louisa's second marriage was to Charles Derwig on September 5, 1906.	Henry Horstman and Louisa Horstman were married on 30 April 1890 in the German Methodist Episcopal Church, Schenectady, NY, by Rev. J.C.Deininger. Source: Faith United Methodist Church, Schenectady, N.Y.

Children of this marriage	Birth date & place	Death date, place & burial place	Marriage date, place & spouse
Jessie L.	1891 Schenectady, NY	8 February 1900 Schenectady, NY (Vale Cemetery)	N/A
Clarence E.	25 June 1894 Schenectady, NY	15 January 1978 Enfield, CT	(unknown-changed name to Charles Forstmann)
Irene	January 1897 Schenectady, NY	(unknown)	Married Harry J. Service in Schenectady, N.Y.
Raymond Henry	3 January 1900 Schenectady, NY	1 December 1989 Schenectady, NY (Vale Cemetery)	Married Jean Allyn Douglass on July 10, 1937 in Ilion, NY
Elmer Roy	June 1902 Schenectady, NY	7 January 1908 Schenectady, NY (Vale Cemetery)	N/A

Christian Friedrich Horstmann	Birth date: 21 April 1832
Full birth name of husband	Birth place: #29 Hille, Kreis Minden, Prussia
Carl Heinrich Horstmann	
His father	Death date: 24 January 1897
Marie Elizabeth Kleine	Death place: Hille, Kreis Minden, Prussia
His mother with maiden name	
	Burial place: Hille Friedhof

Caroline Marie Kasten	Birth date: 25 June 1839
Full maiden name of wife	Birth place: # 9 Eickhorst, Kreis Minden, Prussia
Carl Heinrich Kasten	
Her father	Death date: 24 February 1894
Ann Kolling	Death place: Hille, Kreis Minden, Prussia
Her mother with maiden name	
	Burial place: Hille Friedhof

Comments	Marriage date, place, etc.
Information compiled from records of Hille Evangelische Kirche and Schenectady, NY city records. Family photograph in Chapter One courtesy of Elizabeth Buhrmester.	Married 29 April 1859 in the Hille Evangelische Kirche Source: Church records.

Children of this marriage	Birth date & place	Death date, place & burial place	Marriage date, place & spouse
Caroline Marie Louisa	24 December 1859 #29 Hille	10 January 1935	21 January 1882 Carl Husz
Christian Heinrich August	25 September 1861 #29 Hille	23 July 1926	November 1893 Marie Schutte
Heinrich Christian	21 October 1863 #29 Hille	7 October 1903 Schenectady, NY (Vale Cemetery)	30 April 1890 Louisa Horstmann in Schenectady, N.Y.
Friedrich Wilhelm	1 November 1865 #29 Hille	1 December 1909 Schenectady, NY (Vale Cemetery)	ca. 1890 Rose Gerding In Schenectady, NY
Carl August	15 November 1867 #29 Hille	10 March 1870	N/A
Caroline Marie Sophie	4 October 1869 #29 Hille	8 December 1871	N/A

Caroline Marie Sophie	15 February 1872 #29 Hille	married Heinrich Becker in 1894, died 1951
Marie Sophie	14 September 1873 #29 Hille	married xxxxx Korff, died 1903
Caroline Marie	3 July 1875 #29 Hille	died 21 December 1876
Frederika Elizabeth	17 September 1876 #29 Hille	died 30 April 1877
Marie Frederika	16 April 1878 #29 Hille	married Heinrich Dreyer, died 1946
Marie Louisa	21 March 1880 #29 Hille	died 1885

(Format from *The Unpuzzling Your Past Workbook* by Emily Anne Croom.)

VITAL RECORDS OF HILLE
(Nordrhein-Westfalen, Germany)

Parish: Evangel. Lutheran

Kirchenkreis: Minden

Filmed at: Landeskirchenamt Bielefeld (1965)
              by L.D.S. Genealogical Society of
              Salt Lake City, Utah

Microfilm No.	Type of Records	Period
470, 451	births	1859-1875
470, 450	deaths	1853-1884
470, 449	births	1847-1858
470, 448	deaths	1885-1916
470, 447	births	1820-1866
470, 446	marriages	1820-1929
470, 445	deaths	1820-1852
470, 444	births, marriages, deaths	1816-1823
470, 595	births, marriages, deaths	1812-1815
470, 594	births, marriages, deaths	1811-1812*
470, 593	births, marriages, deaths	1808-1809
470, 592	births, marriages, deaths	1774-1808
470, 591	births, marriages, deaths	1725-1773**

*   partially in French

**   poor quality

BIBLIOGRAPHY

Books

Adams, Willi Paul. *The German-Americans: An Ethnic Experience* (American Edition). Indianapolis: Indiana University-Purdue University at Indianapolis, 1993.

Aldrich, Mark. *Safety First: Technology, Labor and Business in the Building of American Work Safety, 1870–1939.* Baltimore and London: Johns Hopkins University Press, 1997.

Aldrich, Mark. *Death Rode the Rails: American Railroad Accidents and Safety, 1828–1965.* Baltimore: The Johns Hopkins University Press, 2006.

Allen, Leslie. *Liberty: the Statue and the American Dream.* New York: The Statue of Liberty-Ellis Island Foundation, Inc., 1985.

Bazelon, Bruce S. *Horstmanns: The Enterprise of Military Equipage*, REF Typesetting & Publishing, Inc., Manassas, Virginia, 1997

Beard, Patricia. *After the Ball.* New York: HarperCollins Publishers, Inc., 2003.

Beebe, Lucius. *High Iron.* New York: Bonanza Books, A Division of Crown Publishers, Inc., 1938.

Botkin, B.A. and Alvin F. Harlow, editors. *A Treasury of Railroad Folklore.* New York: Bonanza Books, 1953.

Brands, H.W. *The Reckless Decade: America in the 1890s.* Chicago and London: The University of Chicago Press, 1995.

Brownstone, David M., Irene M. Franck, and Douglass Brownstone. *Island of Hope, Island of Tears.* New York: Barnes & Noble Books, 1979.

Burrows, Edwin G, and Mike Wallace. *Gotham: A History of New York City to 1898.* New York: Oxford University Press, 1999.

Clarke, Thomas Curtis, et.al. *The American Railway*. New York: Bramhall House, 1888.

Craig, Gordon A. *Germany 1866–1945*. New York: Oxford University Press, 1978.

Daniels, Roger. *Coming to America: A History of Immigration and Ethnicity in American Life (Second Edition)*. New York: HarperCollins, 2002.

Depew, Chauncey M. *My Memories of 80 Years*. New York: Scribner's Sons, 1922.

Depew, Chauncey M. *Life and Later Speeches of Chauncey M. Depew*. Rahway, New Jersey: The Cassell Publishing Co., 1894.

Dodds, John W. *Everyday Life in Twentieth Century America*. New York: G.P. Putnam's Sons, 1965.

Edson, William D. and H.L. Vail, Jr. *Steam Locomotives of the New York Central Lines, Part 1: New York Central and Hudson River R.R.* Cleveland, Ohio: New York Central System Historical Society, Inc., March 1997.

Ely, James W., Jr. *Railroads and American Law*. University Press of Kansas, 2001.

Eyck, Erich. *Bismarck and the German Empire*. New York: W.W. Norton & Company, Inc., 1950.

Faust, Albert Bernhardt. *The German Element in the United States*. New York: The Steuben Society of America, 1927.

Feuchtwanger, E.J. *Prussia: Myth and Reality—The Role of Prussia in German History*. Chicago: Henry Regnery Company, 1970.

Finney, Jack. *Time and Again*. New York: Scribner Paperback Fiction, Simon & Schuster, Inc., 1970.

Gamst, Frederick C. *The Hoghead: an Industrial Ethnology of the Locomotive Engineer*. Case Studies in Cultural Anthropology. New York: Holt, Rinehart and Winston, 1980.

Garratt, Colin and Max Wade-Matthews. *Illustrated Book of Steam and Rail*. New York: Barnes & Noble, 2003.

Gatzke, Hans W. *Germany and the United States—"A Special*

Relationship?" Cambridge, Massachusetts, and London, England: Harvard University Press, 1980.

Grafenstein, Heinrich. *Minden: Die Stadt an der Weser.* Minden: J.C.C. Bruns Verlag, undated.

Handlin, Oscar. *A Pictorial History of Immigration.* New York: Crown Publishers, Inc., 1972.

Handlin, Oscar. *The Uprooted.* New York: Grosset & Dunlap, 1951.

Handlin, Oscar. *The Uprooted* (Second Edition Enlarged). Boston, Toronto: Little Brown & Company, 1973.

Harlow, Alvin F. *The Road of the Century.* Toronto: McClelland and Stewart, Ltd., 1947.

Hart, Larry. *Schenectady: A Pictorial History.* Scotia, New York: Old Dorp Books, 1984.

Hart, Larry. *Schenectady's Golden Era: 1880–1930.* Scotia, New York: Old Dorp Books, 1974.

Hart, Larry. *Tales of Old Schenectady (Volume II: The Changing Scene).* Scotia, New York: Old Dorp Books, 1977.

Hill, Howard G. *Riding the Limiteds' Locomotives.* Seattle: Superior Publishing Company, 1972.

Hoobler, Dorothy and Thomas. *The German American Family Album.* New York: Oxford University Press, 1996.

Hoyt, Edwin P. *The Vanderbilts and Their Fortunes.* Garden City, New York: Doubleday & Company, Inc., 1962.

Hubbard, Freeman H. *Railroad Avenue: Great Stories and Legends of American Railroading.* New York: McGraw-Hill Book Company, Inc., 1945.

Hungerford, Edward. *Men and Iron: The History of New York Central.* New York: Thomas Y. Crowell Company, 1938.

Johnson, Anna C. *Peasant Life in Germany.* New York, 1859.

Jones, Maldwyn A. *Destination America.* New York: Holt, Rinehart, and Winston, 1976.

Josephson, Matthew. *Edison: a Biography.* New York: McGraw-Hill Book Company, Inc., 1959.

Kamphoefner, Walter D., Wolfgang Helbich, and Ulrike Sommer, editors. *News from the Land of Freedom: German Immigrants Write Home*. Ithaca, NY, and London: Cornell University Press, 1991.

Klein, Aaron E. *The History of the New York Central System*. Greenwich, Connecticut: Brompton Books Corporation, 1985.

La Follette, Belle Case (Vol. 1) and Fola La Follette (Vol. 2). *Robert M. La Follette, 1855–1925*. New York: McMillan Co., 1953.

Licht, Walter. *Working for the Railroad: The organization of work in the Nineteenth Century*. Princeton University Press, 1983.

Marzio, Peter C., ed. *A Nation of Nations*, Smithsonian Institution. New York: Harper & Row, 1976.

Moreno, Barry. *Images of America: Castle Garden and Battery Park*. Charleston, South Carolina: Arcadia Publishing, 2007.

Morris, Charles R. *The Tycoons*. New York: Henry Holt and Company, 2005.

Ogburn, Charlton. *Railroads: The Great American Adventure*. National Geographic Society, 1977.

Orr, John W. *Set up Running: The Life of a Pennsylvania Railroad Engineman*. University Park, Pennsylvania: The Pennsylvania State University Press, 2001.

Painter, Nell Irvin. *Standing at Armageddon: The United States 1877–1919*. New York and London: W.W. Norton & Company, 1987.

Phillips, David Graham. *The Treason of the Senate*. Stanford, California: Academic Reprints (reprint of Cosmopolitan Magazine, Vol. XL, No. 5, March 1906).

Reed, Robert C. *Train Wrecks: A Pictorial History of Accidents on the Main Line*. Atglen, Pennsylvania: Schiffer Publishing, Ltd., 1996.

Reeves, Pamela. *Ellis Island—Gateway to the American Dream*. New York: Barnes & Noble Books, 2002.

Reinhardt, Richard. *Workin' on the Railroad: Reminiscences from the Age of Steam*. Norman, Oklahoma: University of Oklahoma Press, 2003.

Renehan, Edward J., Jr. *Commodore—The Life of Cornelius Vanderbilt*. New York: Basic Books, 2007.

Richardson, Reed C. *The Locomotive Engineer, 1863–1963: A*

Century of Railway Labor Relations and Work Rules. Ann Arbor, Michigan: University of Michigan, Graduate School of Business Administration, 1963.

Riechmann, Wolfgang. *Vivat Amerika: Auswanderung aus dem Kreis Minden 1816–1933.* Minden, Germany: Mindener Geschichtsverein, 1993.

Riis, Jacob. *How the Other Half Lives.* New York: Charles Scribner's Sons, 1890.

Schneirov, Richard, Sheldon Stromquist, and Nick Salvatore, editors. *The Pullman Strike and the Crisis of the 1890s.* Urbana and Chicago: University of Illinois Press, 1999.

Seaton, Albert. *The Army of the German Empire, 1870–1888.* Great Britain: Osprey Publishing Ltd., 1973.

Sinclair, Angus. *Locomotive Engine Running and Management.* Seventeenth Edition, 1890.

Sturmer, Michael. *The German Century.* New York: Barnes & Noble, 2001.

Stromquist, Shelton. *A Generation of Boomers: The Pattern of Labor Conflict in Nineteenth-Century America.* Urbana and Chicago: University of Illinois Press, 1993.

Sullivan, Mark. *Our Times: The United States 1900–1925 (Vol.III, Pre-War America).* New York and London: Charles Scribner's Sons, 1930.

Thompson, Anthony W. and Robert J. Church, eds. *Railroad History in Photographs: 150 Years of North American Railroading.* Wilton, CA: Signature Press, 1996.

Vanderbilt, Arthur T., II. *Fortune's Children.* New York: William Morrow and Company, Inc., 1989.

Walker, Mack. *Germany and the Emigration 1816–1885.* Cambridge, MA: Harvard University Press, 1964.

Wall, Robert. *Ocean Liners.* New York. E.P. Dutton, 1977.

White, John H., Jr. *The American Railroad Freight Car from the Wood-Car Era to the Coming of Steel.* Baltimore and London: The Johns Hopkins University Press, 1993.

Withuhn, William L. *The Spirit of Steam: The Golden Age of North American Steam*. New York: Barnes & Noble Books, 2003.

Zimmermann, Karl R. *Twentieth Century Limited*. St. Paul, MN: MBI Publishing Company, 2002.

Newspapers

"Shipwrecked and Storm-Beaten." *New York Times*, April 23, 1881.

"Marine Intelligence." *New York Times*, April 23, 1881.

"The Flow of Immigration." *New York Times*, April 22, 1881.

"A Scene in Castle Garden." *Harper's Weekly*, February 2, 1889.

"German Methodist Church History." *Schenectady Union Star*, June 26, 1924.

"The Latest Railroad Disaster." *Harper's Weekly*, January 21, 1882.

"City's Rate of Growth Hit Peak in 1900-10." *Schenectady Union-Star*, June 26, 1948.

"Powderly to the People." *New York Times*, August 22, 1890.

"A Surprising Revelation." *Olean Weekly Democrat*, October 24, 1889.

"Depew Led in Prayer." *Herald and Torch Light (Hagerstown, Maryland)*, November 27, 1890.

"Mr. Depew to Railroad Men." *New York Times*, February 25, 1899.

"State Railroad Commission Report." New York Times, January 13, 1902.

"Engineer Fell From Locomotive." *Schenectady Daily Union*, October 3, 1903.

"Engineer Horstman Badly Hurt." *Amsterdam Evening Recorder*, October 5, 1903.

"Schenectady Man Injured." *Schenectady Gazette*, October 5, 1903.

"Horstman Is Dead." *Schenectady Daily Union*, October 8, 1903.

"Both Lived in Same House." *Schenectady Gazette*, October 9, 1903.

"Train Ran Miles Without Engineer." *Albany Times Union*, October 8, 1903.

"Fatigue puts rail workers on a dangerous track." *Houston Chronicle,* August 9, 2005.

"Who is the Murderer?" *Washington Post,* December 27, 1904.

"Engineer in Wreck was on Duty 33 Hours." *New York Times,* January 5, 1907.

"La Follette Wins After Hard Fight." *Washington Times,* January 11, 1907.

"Law Limiting Hours of Trainmen Passed." *New York Times,* January 10, 1907.

"Depew's Soiled Toga Demanded." *New York Sun,* January 4, 1906.

"Depew Determines to Hold His Job." *New York Times,* April 24, 1910.

"Famous New Yorkers." *Syracuse Post-Standard,* November 9, 2005.

"How Power May Spoil a Leader's Perspective," *Wall Street Journal,* January 31, 2007.

Magazines and Journals

Cable, Mary. "Damned Plague Ships and Swimming Coffins," *American Heritage,* August 1960.

Dougherty, Charles. "The Transatlantic Steamship Captains," *Harpers New Monthly Magazine,* August 1886.

McQueen, William J. "The Making of a Railroad Man," *Saturday Evening Post,* February 1900.

Meeham, Thomas. "Fact or Fable?" *Railroad History,* Spring/Summer 2007 (No. 196).

Moffett, Samuel E. "Our Overworked Railroads," *Collier's Weekly,* January 19, 1907.

Moffit, Cleveland. "At the Throttle," *McClure's Magazine,* September 1893.

Odom, E. Dale. "Chauncey Mitchell Depew." *Encyclopedia of American Business History and Biography: Railroads in the Nineteenth Century,* 1988, pp 90–4.

Parmet, Robert D. "The Presidential Fever of Chauncey Depew,"

Quarterly Journal of the New York State Historical Society, July 1970 (No. 54).

Pascucci, Dr. Robert R. *Electric City Immigrants: Italians and Poles of Schenectady, N.Y., 1880–1930*. Albany, New York: State University of New York, Department of History, 1984.

Phillips, David Graham. "The Treason of the Senate," *Cosmopolitan Magazine*, March 1906 (No. 5).

Reimer, Thomas. "Distant Thunder: The German-American Clergy of Schenectady, New York, and the European War, 1914–1917," *Quarterly Journal of the New York State Historical Association*, July 1992 (No. 3).

Rittner, Don. "Remains of Schenectady's First Water System Found," *Schenectady County Historical Society Newsletter*, September/October 2006.

Wetzel, Kurt. "Railroad Management's Response to Operating Employee Accidents, 1890–1913," Labor History, Summer 1980 (No. 3).

White, John Jr. "Oh, To Be a Locomotive Engineer," *Railroad History*, Spring/Summer 2004 (No. 190).

White, John Jr. "Once It Was Every Boy's Ambition," *Railroad History*, Fall/Winter 2003 (No. 189).

_____."The Ballad of Casey Jones," *Locomotive Engineers Journal*, Winter 1999 (No.4).

_____. "The Death Roll of Industry," *Charities and the Commons*, February 2, 1907.

_____. "A Sea Captain's Day's Work," *World's Work Magazine*, April 1901.

_____. "Before Castle Garden, Ellis Island," *American History Illustrated*, September/October 1990.

Other Sources

Encyclopedia of North American Railroads (eds. Middleton, William D., George M. Smerk, and Roberta L. Diehl). Bloomington, Indiana: Indiana University Press, 2007.

German Emigration Center. "Das Buch zum Deutschen Auswandererhaus" (edition DAH), Bremerhaven, Germany, 2006.

Licefa Company. "100 Jahre Licefa. Ein Unternehmen schreibt Geschichte (1907-2007)." Bad Salzuflen, Germany, 2008.

McDonald, Charles W. "The Federal Railroad Safety Program: 100 Years of Safer Railroads." U.S. Department of Transportation, Washington, D.C.: August 1993.

National Railway Historical Society (Rochester Chapter). "The Water Level Route," Second Ed., 1984.

National Railway Publication Co., "Official Guide of the Railways," New York Central & Hudson River Railroads, October 1903.

New York Central and Hudson River Railroad Company. "Rules of the Operating Department." January 19, 1908.

New York Central and Hudson River Railroad Company. Annual Reports of the Board of Directors to Stockholders, 1897-1903.

New York State Board of Railroad Commissioners. Annual Report. Albany, New York, January 11, 1904.

Reimer, Thomas. "German-American Ethnicity in Albany, N.Y., 1888–1908." M.A. Thesis, State University of New York at Albany, 1988.

Schenectady County Historical Society. "Images of America: Glenville." Chicago: Arcadia Publishing, 2005.

Schenectady County Public Library. "Schenectady Railroad History." Digital History Archive.

Taylor, David A. and Lucinda M. Parker. *Night of Disaster: The New York Central Gulf Curve Wreck*. Utica, New York: Artspace Graphics & Imaging, First Ed., 1989

United States. United States House of Representatives. Fifty-Ninth

Congress, Second Session. Debate on the "Hours of Service Act," Congressional Record, January–March, 1907.

United States. Interstate Commerce Commission. Eighteenth Annual Report. Washington, D.C.: Government Printing Office, December 19, 1904.

United States. Interstate Commerce Commission. Nineteenth Annual Report. Washington, D.C.: Government Printing Office, December 14, 1905.

United States. Senate. Fifty-Sixth Congress, Second Session. Debate on the Accident Reports Act, Congressional Record, March 1901.

United States. Senate. Fifty-Ninth Congress, First Session: Debate on the "Hours of Service Act," Congressional Record, June 1906.

United States. Senate. Fifty-Ninth Congress, Second Session. Debate on the "Hours of Service Act," Congressional Record, January–March 1907.

Immigration:
www.amerikanetz.de
www.castlegarden.org
www.dah-bremerhaven.de
www.immigrantships.net
www.theshipslist.com

Railroad history:
www.rlhs.org
www.newyorkcentralsystemhistoricalsociety.org
www.nationalrrmuseum.org
www.ble.org

Schenectady, New York history:
www.schenectadyhistory.org
www.schist.org